ANOTHER WAY IS POSSIBLE
BECOMING A DEMOCRATIC TEACHER IN A STATE SCHOOL

Self-Directed Learning in a Context
Of Democracy, Human Rights and Community

About the book

The author argues that a new "Way" of schooling is required. Young people are 'natural learners' needing time and space to develop their interests and passions, in schools where teachers and students collaborate respecting democracy and human rights. They do not need exam factories. He describes his personal journey leading to the creation of such a learning community in an English state school.

About the author

Derry Hannam has a bachelor's degree in education from Oxford University and an M.Phil. in educational research from Exeter University.

In his twenty years as a teacher in English state secondary schools he always tried to create environments where students could make choices about and take control of their own learning in a democratic and rights respecting context.

Derry has been described as a 'bridge person' who tries to bring about dialogue between the mainly private democratic education movement with its 500+ schools worldwide and state or public school systems. This has at times involved supporting democratic schools in legal actions; a role that he has played in England, Germany, Denmark, and the Netherlands. He is currently supporting start-up democratic schools in several countries, advising them how best to work with their respective state systems.

ANOTHER WAY IS POSSIBLE
BECOMING A DEMOCRATIC TEACHER IN A STATE SCHOOL

Self-Directed Learning in a Context
Of Democracy, Human Rights and Community

By Derry Hannam

Although the publisher and the author have made every effort to ensure that the information in this book was correct at press time and while this publication is designed to provide accurate information in regard to the subject matter covered, the publisher and the author assume no responsibility for errors, inaccuracies, omissions, or any other inconsistencies herein and hereby disclaim any liability to any party for any loss, damage, or disruption caused by errors or omissions, whether such errors or omissions result from negligence, accident, or any other cause.

This book also contains links to external third-party websites, over whose content the author has no influence. Therefore, we cannot accept any liability for this third-party content.

Published by FHREE in assosiation with ALLI asbl
www.fhree.org
www.alliasbl.lu
Cover illustration by: Luke Hannam
Book Layout by: Max Sauber

ISBN: 9798740215945 (paperback)
ISBN: 9780463289334 (ebook)

This work is licensed under a Creative Commons Attribution-NonCommercial-NoDerivatives 4.0 International License

This is a human-readable summary of (and not a substitute for) the license. Disclaimer.
You are free to:
Share — copy and redistribute the material in any medium or format
The licensor cannot revoke these freedoms as long as you follow the license terms.
Under the following terms:
Attribution — You must give appropriate credit, provide a link to the license, and indicate if changes were made. You may do so in any reasonable manner, but not in any way that suggests the licensor endorses you or your use.
NonCommercial — You may not use the material for commercial purposes.
NoDerivatives — If you remix, transform, or build upon the material, you may not distribute the modified material.
No additional restrictions — You may not apply legal terms or technological measures that legally restrict others from doing anything the license permits.
Notices:
You do not have to comply with the license for elements of the material in the public domain or where your use is permitted by an applicable exception or limitation.
No warranties are given. The license may not give you all of the permissions necessary for your intended use. For example, other rights such as publicity, privacy, or moral rights may limit how you use the material.

Contents

INTRODUCTION 1

PART ONE – WHERE DID THE IDEAS COME FROM? 11
Chapter 1 – School 12
Chapter 2 – Work 20
Chapter 3 – Training to be a Teacher 30

PART TWO – BECOMING A DEMOCRATIC TEACHER -
PUTTING THE IDEAS INTO PRACTICE 41
Chapter 4 – My first job as a Teacher of Class 1H 42
Chapter 5 – An amazing piece of synchronicity 45
Chapter 6 – Creating a Democratic Class and Curriculum – Making It Up As We Went Along 49
Chapter 7 – The Democratic Class becomes a Democratic Year Group of seven Classes 72
Chapter 8 – 2H hits the national press – The visit to the SUN 76
Chapter 9 – 2H Teaches the teachers 85
Chapter 10 – Democracy begins to Impact on the Whole School – The School Council 88
Chapter 11 – Jo's Story 100

PART THREE – WHAT WAS IT ALL ABOUT AND WHAT HAS IT GOT TO DO WITH NOW? 105
Chapter 12 – Love and the Public Service Ethic 106
Chapter 13 – The Importance of Democratic Structures and Human Rights 110
Chapter 14 – Non-coercive Relationships and the Importance of Play ... 119
Chapter 15 – Curriculum, Streaming and Selection, Oracy and Literacy, Assessment and Learning 123
Chapter 16 – Education for Citizenship, Human Rights, Sustainability, Entrepreneurship 134

CONCLUSION – Can State Schools today move towards becoming Democratic Learning Communities? 138

AFTERWORD – WHAT DOES IT ALL MEAN FOR THE FUTURE AND THE FOURTH INDUSTRIAL REVOLUTION? 146

NOTES	165
BIBLIOGRAPHY	166

INTRODUCTION

This book tells one story in four parts plus a forward-looking afterword.

The first part describes the journey by which one young person in England, me, became convinced that student-centred learning in a democratic community setting, grounded in respect for the human rights of young people, was what had been missing from my own unrewarding experience of school. It chronicles the experiences that coalesced into beliefs that led me to become a teacher determined to see if 'another way was possible.'

The second part describes how as a newly qualified teacher I tried, in a pragmatic 'make it up as we go along' fashion, to introduce democratic ideas and practices together with self-managed and self-directed learning into a state secondary modern school (**1**) from 1969 to 1971.

These ideas had evolved partly from my own experience and partly from the rich though neglected tradition of English progressive education that I discovered in dusty unread corners of my college library. During its first year the project involved just one mixed gender class of thirty-six eleven-year-olds. In its second year it grew to include all seven classes of the year group while at the same time having a growing influence on the whole school.

The third part reviews the experiences of the story and reflects upon what they meant. It brings the story from the past into the present. It connects with the need to re-imagine the sterile and authoritarian 'exam factory' schools that we have created in many countries as part of what the Finnish educationalist Pasi Sahlberg describes as GERM (Global Education Reform Movement) (Sahlberg, 2015).

The book concludes with a consideration of the extent to which it would it be possible to replicate the story of Class 1H/2H in the climate that exists in English state schools in 2020 under the shadow of the Covid-19 virus.

There could have been a fifth part which might have focused on the critical importance of community. The school as a self-managing community which itself becomes the means whereby the wider community within which the school is set can rediscover and reinvigorate itself. The community school becoming the vehicle by which the wider community 'turns on' to itself. This re-imagined approach grounded not just in the everyday practice of democracy, human rights and self-directed learning but also as community-based centres for creatively exploring sustainability – a theme well developed by Fiona Carnie in 'Rebuilding Our Schools from the Bottom Up' (Carnie, 2018). This is what I tried to do in the next two schools in which I worked but that will have to be another book!

Finally, by way of a forward-looking Afterword, I include a revised and amalgamated version of two keynote talks that I delivered to the European Democratic Education Community (EUDEC) conference in Crete in August 2018 and in Kiev in August 2019. In it I begin to develop a rationale that argues for a synergy between the positive messages and collective experience of democratic education, exemplified by the practice in several hundred already existing democratic schools around the world, and the tsunami of change represented by the interconnected technological developments of the Fourth Industrial Revolution.

The four ideas of democracy, human rights, community and sustainability are interdependent and will become more so. The collision between an infinite growth model of capitalism and a planet of finite resources, set in a finely balanced slowly evolved eco-system on which it makes its predatory demands, is happening now. David Attenborough of 'Blue Planet' fame gives us only ten years to correct global warming and prevent unmanageable climate change.

Also happening right now is a rapid growth of socio-economic inequality with its attendant growth of political instability as exemplified by Trumpism and Brexit and compounded by the arrival of the Covid-19 virus. The planet needs a generation of young people who have learned how to live together peacefully, how to manage the stresses of community, how to share and to respect interdependence and diversity, how to cultivate creativity and problem solving, and how to explore sustainability in the everyday shared management of their schools. They need to be able to take responsibility for the direction of their own learning and their own lives, for defining who and what they are and want to become. They will need to be able to create their own identities and not rely on that provided by fast disappearing paid employment.

We need to learn from what is already beginning to happen in the five hundred or so democratic schools worldwide which represent 'pioneers of possibility' that are already showing the way. In these schools, young people learn to redefine 'work' as what they want to do and what they are good at, and what creates 'community.' They learn to believe in and cultivate their own genius. It is from this kind of environment that the 1-2% needed to create and develop the technological advances of the Fourth Industrial

Revolution will also be found who will at the same time have learned from their school experience to respect democracy and human rights as well as to cultivate their own genius.

My project was an attempt to create what might now be described as a Democratic Learning Community. It took place at the time of the formation of the Club of Rome, and two years before the publication of its seminal work 'Limits to Growth' (Meadows, 1972) which has now sold over 30 million copies. It was just before the oil crisis of 1973. There were three beliefs motivating the project, though the need to create a sustainable world in the school and on the planet was not one of them. It would be now however and I would argue that such a democratic learning community provides the best possible opportunity to educate for sustainability!

The three organising ideas behind my project were, first, that it should demonstrate an intrinsic respect for and trust in young people as individual human beings with an inherent capacity for learning, in a way that conventional authoritarian schooling did not. Second, that the ideas would enhance learning through rebuilding the confidence of the children who had just experienced the trauma of failing the high-stakes '11+ examination.' Third, that they would provide an experiential preparation for life in a democratic society.

Teacher coercion was to be reduced to as near to zero as possible while student freedom, choice and responsibility were to be maximised. The curriculum was to be negotiated around the curiosity and interests of the students and wherever possible learning was to be collaborative. Asking questions was to be encouraged while fear of 'getting the wrong answer' was to be eliminated. The management of the overall learning environment would as much as possible be in the hands of a 'class meeting', operated with one person one vote, on the understanding that teacher intervention would be necessary if anyone was put at risk of harm, or if neighbouring classes were at risk of being disrupted.

I was prepared to be fired if necessary, but having married young with three young children and a mortgage to pay when I left university, I aimed to survive in the school system for as long as possible, if only so that the ideas could be given a fair chance to succeed. I was determined to work in the state system although some tempting posts were available in private schools. After all the state system was where most of the kids were including all the kids from backgrounds like mine – and my own children.

Inspiration to write this book came from the US educational writer Alfie

Kohn (1999 and 2013). It is Kohn's view that educators whose experience leads them to challenge the status quo and develop innovative approaches that circumvent it should interrogate their own formative experiences to develop an understanding of why they think as they do. What has led them to develop practices that diverge from conventional authoritarian regimes for state schools? To seek alternatives to their emphasis on a narrow prescriptive curriculum, authoritarian directive teaching, competitive individualised learning, obsessive 'measuring what can easily be measured' grades/marks, high stakes testing and relentless target setting and data collection - with little scope for student choice, creativity, collaboration or intrinsic motivation.

At the time of writing, this book might well be located in the literature of 'student voice.' This concept has gained momentum and status in recent years in the English-speaking world though I do not particularly like the expression 'student voice.' The 'voice' may or may not be heard. Even if it is heard there is no guarantee that the voices of all will be either expressed or heard through the more or less representative structures usually involved in the student councils common in English or US state schools. I prefer to describe the processes described in this book as 'student participation in decision making' when concerned with individual learning choices, and 'student participation in democratic decision making' when concerned with collective class or school decision making.

It will become clear to the reader that this extends beyond the articulation of 'voice' to include decision making and action, often negotiation and sharing responsibility with adults, together with reflection upon and evaluation of outcomes. Most important of all it involves everyone as a participant. The territory within which decisions are made should, and did in my case, include what conventionally might be described as curriculum, extra-curriculum and social organization though I regarded them as being part of a seamless whole. In fact, it involved the creation of what might now be termed a 'democratic learning community' with an emphasis less on adjustment and 'fitting in' and more on learning to create and control change.

This book challenges the tendency of schools to assert the incapacity of children which too often just adds to a similar tendency on the part of parents. When reinforced by 'failure' in the eleven plus examination, as was the experience of the children of this book, the sense of incapacity was passed on to the children themselves. They learn to deny their own capabilities and lose the will to resist those who would diminish them.

My work with the young people of class 1H/2H stood totally opposed to this. It set out to restore their lost confidence, creativity, and the sense of authenticity of their existing feelings and knowledge. To restore their right to speak from the heart and not just to say what was believed to be expected by authority. All set in a context of as much freedom as was possible within the limitations of a state school.

We have fought two world wars to defend democracy but we do not yet have a society of equal opportunity for UK young people from all social backgrounds regardless of the financial and social capital of their parents. Our private schools are held up to be models of excellence in contrast to the failure of the state schools. There is in fact no basis for this belief. The academic achievement of the private schools attended by seven per cent of the population, is no better than would be expected given the socially advantaged backgrounds of the students that attend them. The remaining ninety-three per cent of us are taught to believe that this is the natural order of things by a largely sycophantic media.

This divided school system and all that flows from it is not the basis for a good or just society and I did not become a teacher in order to perpetuate this nonsense. I became a teacher in order to inspire young people to work towards the creation of a society that would offer opportunities for all its young people to grow and learn, to contribute whatever their individual special talents have to offer for their own well-being and the well-being of others.

In England schools today are being occupied by an army of 'behaviour management consultants' 'expert' in rewards, punishments and sanctions. They are making the curriculum more 'rigorous' to the point of making it incomprehensible to many children and then insisting on separating the students into 'streams' of fast and slow learners while setting targets for test scores upon which teachers' salaries and job security depend – all contrary to established research findings. The mix is toxic and destructive of the well-being of teachers as well as their students. It is sustained by the pernicious link between politicians and for-profit examination companies who in the name of 'maintaining standards' ensure that the same proportion of young people 'fail' every year however hard they try.

The key group in creating an effective environment for learning in a school are first and foremost motivated and engaged students themselves. Teachers and parents provide a very important context, followed closely by the wider community and general social environment of the school. Central government, in the shape of curriculum prescribers, test designers, behaviour management consultants and inspectors, are nearly always a negative influence on the motivation of school students. Especially when they are victims of lobbying sharks from the big multi-national textbook and testing companies. Providing young people with the opportunity and freedom to find and pursue their own interests as far as they can is much more important.

The school staff need to understand young people, to be responsive to the interests and experiences of the students while being passionately interested in aspects of the world themselves. They need to know what it means to be a motivated self-starting and self-directing learner now and not just from memories of the past. As Goya put it when he was in his eighties 'Aun aprendo' – 'I still learn.' Ideally this would apply not just to the teachers but to caretakers, secretaries, coaches, technicians, cooks and librarians. All the adults in the school community share this responsibility. They all need to consistently model what a motivated learner looks like, to be people who are interested in the world as a whole and the welfare of its human and non-human inhabitants. Young human beings are, to paraphrase Jerome Bruner, by nature curious and collaborative learners who revel in becoming competent in many ways (Bruner, 1960 and 1966). Only if these natural human traits are obstructed and impelled to disengage in poor school or home environments will young people not be avid learners.

Inevitably every young person will have off-days. Those from frustrating and unloving homes may well have many of them. So long as the majority have not had their will to learn fatally damaged, as failure in the eleven plus examination can come close to achieving, children can cope with the off-days of others especially if they have the opportunity to participate in the creation and operation of democratic structures designed to do so. Given this opportunity they will also acquire the skills and understanding required to share in the support and management of their 'off-day' peers.

My forty years work in and with schools and school students has been dedicated to the exploration of ways in which such learning environments can be created, in collaboration with the young people themselves. It is my experience that this collaboration is crucial for the creation of a school environment which stimulates, encourages and supports learners. An environment in which learning could flourish in a 'play democracy' that fostered the 'true self' of the child in such a way that all the curiosity, motivation to learn, creativity, empathy and spontaneity possessed by each student would be at work (Gray, 2013). This involved developing a new kind of relationship between teacher and student that did not rely on traditional authoritarian methods which I believed cultivated the 'false self' of the child in ways that were not conducive to effective learning.

The project was in many ways amazingly successful. In other ways it was less successful, in particular in my failure to communicate what I was doing to the school staff as a whole. Although in the second year of the project a number of young teachers, and one not so young who was also a parent, chose to join the team others became overtly anxious and a few hostile.

After two years I was head-hunted to become head of a large humanities department in a large new purpose-built school in a neighbouring county. Later I became a head of house and still later deputy head in a third school eventually becoming acting head teacher during the prolonged illness of the head teacher. I took the model of democratic learning community with me to each new post but it was the first two years covered in this book that provided the most vivid and unforgettable experience.

It would be almost impossible to imagine that a young teacher in the first year of their career could have such opportunities for doing things in a different way and playfully making it up as we went along in these more prescribed and constrained times for teachers. However, whenever I speak with young teachers I always argue that if you are attracted to the ideas of self-directed learning and democratic education then whatever your situation it is always possible to do something of a more playful, participative and democratic nature. Certainly, the concept of 'student voice' that has emerged in the last twenty years provides some cover as did the 'developing skills of participation and responsible action' aspects of the citizenship education component of the English national curriculum from 2001 to 2010 (QCA 2000).

The writing has been enriched by an extraordinary piece of synchronicity. While working on the first of the chapters on 1H/2H, my first class, one of the ex-students appeared on my Facebook page. He was nearly 60 years old and about to retire as a deputy head teacher. I had not heard from him for some 45 years. He had some vivid recollections of being in the democratic learning community for two years between the age of eleven and thirteen. He managed to assemble a group of alumni who have contributed to the book either orally or, in two cases, with written recollections.

After 20 years of teaching in schools my work took me into the world of school inspection. My career as an Ofsted (2) inspector came to an end when I worked with others against the inspectorate on behalf of the small but very democratic Summerhill School which Ofsted was attempting to close in 1999-2000. Fortunately, we were successful in the subsequent court case and Ofsted's demands were rejected by the court (Cunningham et.al. 2000). As far as I know this is the only time that Ofsted has been successfully resisted in court. The school was re-inspected by Ofsted some ten years later and found to be a 'good school with outstanding features.' Something had changed in those ten years and it wasn't the school! Following this probably mistaken new and relatively short-lived career as an inspector I rediscovered my democratic educator's roots and became an adviser in education for democratic citizenship to several NGOs, the UK government, the Council of Europe and many school student organisations across Europe – especially in the Nordic countries of Norway, Denmark and Finland. This includes working with varying degrees of success to defend democratic schools from uncomprehending regulatory regimes in several other countries and participating in the creation of alternative accountability systems in some more.

The book concludes with qualified and cautious optimism. The final chapters, conclusion and afterword draw together the growing awareness that most of our current school systems are failing the students, the economy, the good society, the future itself, with an attempt to clarify just what the ideas behind the project really were and to give them some justification in the work of educational theorists and researchers. They outline and amalgamate the ways in which creative alternatives already exist in some state schools despite the overall negativity of the political and inspectorial regime within which they have to function.

It then looks more widely at the growing international network of democratic schools that already provide models of how learning environments can be created that offer children space and time to be creative and to realise that creativity into innovative projects. Places where motivation is intrinsic, learning is self-directed and passionately purposeful. Places where the entrepreneurial spirit is fostered in both its social and economic possibilities.

We need to nurture and learn from these schools and learning centres. We will learn nothing if they are inspected to death as was attempted with Summerhill in 1999. The inflexible approach shown by the government of Bavaria recently in its closure of the beautiful and flourishing Ammersee Sudbury School is very depressing. It has damaged the lives of 45 young people whose parents had moved from all parts of Germany so that their children could attend the school. On the other hand, the emergence of some thirty or more democratic schools in France and five new schools in England gives cautious cause for optimism, as does the real possibility that the Dutch network of fifteen such schools might receive state funding in the near future.

PART ONE –

WHERE DID THE IDEAS COME FROM?

Chapter 1 – School

When I was at school children were given virtually no power to control any part of their learning. As a result, I learned almost nothing of lasting value at either primary or secondary school, though I did learn to be very afraid of making mistakes.

I could read well, do basic arithmetic and play the piano in a self-taught fashion before going to school. I learned German by staying with Austrian friends whereas I learned to be afraid to speak a word of French although I got high marks in school tests. My schooling justified the comment 'It is almost impossible to stop children learning but schools manage it somehow.' Learning about democracy or human rights would have been like reading holiday brochures in prison. We had no say whatever in what we learned, who we learned it with, how we learned it, where we learned it and were certainly not encouraged to ask 'why' about anything.

From the age of eight we were 'streamed' by 'intelligence' and told that the 'bright' ones would get to grammar school. This separated me from most of my friends as my Dad was a bus driver while most of the 'top stream' kids were from professional families. At the age of ten I moved into Miss Gunn's 'top' stream class. It was emphasised how lucky I was as she always got nearly all her class 'through the scholarship.' The 'scholarship' being the 11+ (eleven plus) test that selected around 10-15% of children for grammar school and possibly university, a further 10-15% to technical school if there was one in the area (often there was not), while the rest went to secondary modern schools en route to manual labour or factory work of some kind.

There were three streams. The 'top' stream children were nearly all from the larger detached houses and bungalows in the area occupied by the families of middle-class professionals. There were also a few like me from owner occupied but poorly built smaller terraced and semi-detached houses which some working-class families with a little capital had been able to buy just before the second world war. I remember that some of my better off friends had cars and all had televisions and lots of books. My family had none of these though we did have an old upright piano, a few encyclopedias, dictionaries and atlases though no novels.

Children from my kind of background made up the whole of the middle stream who were told that if they worked hard although they would probably not 'pass the scholarship' they would probably get places at the local 'technical' school where they would 'learn a trade'.

The 'bottom' stream almost all came from the local council municipal housing estate and went to the local secondary modern school where most left at fourteen for the then plentiful unskilled jobs. It was very clear to me at an early age that this selection by so-called 'intelligence' was in fact selection by what kind of house you lived in and what your father did for his work. Selection by 'intelligence' merely replicated social class and was basically unfair.

It was while I was at primary school that I became aware that there was another whole class of schools which existed in some mysterious parallel reality to mine of which I would never be a part. My mother cleaned our local church and the houses of some well-off parishioners. I was allowed to play with some of their children until they went off to residential preparatory or 'prep' schools (3) at seven or thereabouts. One 'friend', Martin, went to his prep school as a day boy before disappearing to the very expensive Westminster 'public' (elite private) school at 13. I vividly remember Martin telling me what his parents said when he asked them why I could not have my name put down for Westminster School as well as him. They explained to him that because I was 'poor' I had to go to a 'council school' because there would be no room for all the poor children at Westminster or the other 'good' schools. Outer darkness!

It reminds me now of stories of black children being allowed to play with white children in apartheid South Africa until it was time for the serious racial socialisation of schooling to begin. At the age of about eight I became an avid reader of 'Biggles' books about fighter pilots in the first and second world wars. It dawned on me that to be a Biggles, the fighter pilot officer who did all the brave and exciting flying, you had to have attended one of these alternative reality 'public' schools. People like me would be the 'Gingers' who carried out Biggles' orders, cleaned his boots, fetched his breakfast, and looked after his aeroplane. I suppose Freire (1970) would say I was becoming 'conscientised' (conscientizacao) into an understanding of how power and privilege worked in England; and I knew that I didn't like it and would fight against it as an adult. Or even as a schoolboy if I had the chance!

My father was an unhappy but skilled bus driver who had once owned his own small and totally unsuccessful bus company in Dublin. He told me that if I did what I was told, accepted my powerlessness and boredom now and went to grammar school then I would 'get on.' 'Getting on' meant getting to a place where you worked indoors and were not ordered around by bus inspectors and managers who addressed you by your surname, and 'flippertygibbet girls in offices' who had carpet on their canteen floor. The drivers and conductors had linoleum on their canteen floor which my father interpreted as a sign of the demeaning disrespect in which they, the workers who actually kept the buses running, were held by management or 'authority.'

The point of education in his view was to get to a workplace where there were carpets on the floor, where you had some control over your own working life, were paid a monthly salary rather than a weekly wage, and where nobody could address you by your surname alone. This belief in the semiotics of carpets resonated with me years later when I met Geoff Cooksey, the inspirational first head teacher of the innovative Stantonbury Campus schools. He explained to me that the key to the kind of relationships he was aiming for in 'schools of the future like Stantonbury' were 'Christian names and carpets Derry, Christian names and carpets.'

I clearly remember wondering at the age of ten why the 'bottom' stream put up with schooling when they had virtually no chance of 'getting on' and having carpets on their workplace floors. I presumed that they were too stupid to think about it. Now, of course, the once plentiful unskilled jobs that they were 'schooled' for are fast disappearing. More recently those that remain are being taken by more motivated and less well paid Eastern European immigrants – until the self-inflicted wound of Brexit finally fulfils its promise that is!

I have only one primary school recollection of being able to study something that I was interested in that was not prescribed by the school. This was when Miss Gunn allowed us to read books from the class library for the last half-hour of Friday afternoons. Given one foot in the door of doing something that I had chosen to do and was interested in gave me the opportunity to push it a little further open.

On the whole the class library was pretty thin on subjects of interest to ten-year-old boys but it did have one book on the Royal Navy in the second world war. I was obsessed with the subject having an uncle who had served on the battleship HMS King George V. I regularly borrowed heaps of books from the public library full of unintelligible technical data but also wonderful pictures and fascinating maps of naval engagements. Top of the list was 'Jane's Book of Fighting Ships.' I looked up hundreds of words that I did not understand in dictionaries. I must have known the calibre and range of every gun on every ship in the navy. I could have passed the most advanced test of primary, secondary and anti-aircraft naval armament.

I asked Miss Gunn if we could bring library books from home to read on Friday afternoons instead of the uninspiring books in the class library. She agreed 'so long as they are not comics.' I then persuaded several of the most studious girls who were 'favourites' of the teacher to ask if we could have longer for 'free reading time' if we worked extra-hard at preparing for the 11+ scholarship tests on which her reputation with parents was built. To my surprise she agreed to this too and the half-hour became a whole hour.

Unfortunately, I have no similar recollections of having any choice about anything at grammar school apart from whether to study Latin or German in the second year and Greek or Art in the third. Both these choices were made by my father. He wanted me to do Latin partly in case I might want to be a doctor or a priest and partly because nobody should want to learn how to communicate with Germans. I remember bitterly resenting the question 'and what does your father do' when I told the headmaster that I wanted to go into the Latin class. Afterwards I thought I should have either replied 'What's that got to do with whether I learn Latin or not' instead of meekly saying 'he drives the 47 bus that I come to school on.'

I told my father about this question which I was asked again when I opted for Greek a year later. He admitted then that I had been chosen for interview for a free place at a local expensive public school, Dulwich College, following my 11+ 'scholarship' result but that he had refused to complete the necessary form because the first question was 'father's occupation?' He claims to have written 'none of your fecking business,' or something similar and even more offensive than the Irish version. Strangely, I did not get the place.

Even at the grammar school, which in my area only took ten per cent of the local eleven-year-olds, we were once again streamed by 'intelligence.'. There were the two 'top' language classes, some of whom were expected to 'stay on' into the sixth form (4) to prepare for university, and the two 'bottom' practical classes who were all expected to leave at sixteen at the end of the fifth year. I had come more or less top of my class in every subject in the first year but by the third was wobbling along near the bottom of my top stream class. I received many complaints from teachers about my lack of attention in class but no enquiries at all about the deterioration in the happiness of my home life.

Needless to say, I and most of my 'clever' working class friends, were not selected for the sixth form or university and anyway my father wanted me to be at work 'earning my keep.' So much for choosing Latin so that I could be a doctor or Greek to be a priest!!!

One of my most powerful memories of grammar school is of the relentless bullying about which absolutely nothing was done by staff. On the contrary some of the biggest bullies seemed to be selected to be prefects (5). They must have learned from the staff that power was there to be abused. They were almost entirely the same boys who carried on in the same way as NCOs in the school Air Training Corps Squadron. I joined 1322 Squadron for the free and glorious flying in the tired old Anson and smart little Chipmunks of the RAF Biggin Hill Air Experience Unit.

One of my instructors was an ex-Polish air force sergeant pilot who had fifteen years before flown a spitfire from the same Biggin Hill airfield in the Battle of Britain. He explained that many of his fellow pilots who had fled Poland after the Nazi invasion in 1939 had come from aristocratic backgrounds and had automatically been commissioned as officers into the Royal Air Force but that his father had been a tram driver in Warsaw so he was made a sergeant.

He said it was exactly the same for the British pilots. Those from the elite public schools were automatically commissioned and those from grammar schools flew as sergeants. He was pretty bitter about it all – not least that he was ending his flying career ten years after the end of the war still a sergeant pilot despite having shot down several German bombers. Then, as a final indignity, he was relegated to endless 'circuits and bumps' with air training corps fifteen and sixteen-year-old cadets. His favourite words were 'You want aerobatics today? Maybe it's our last. Let's enjoy it!' Being thrown around the sky by a psychiatrically disturbed but wonderful Polish pilot was unforgettable!

The school prefects had a lot of power. In fact, the whole culture was that of a poor man's imitation of an elite 'public' school, right down to the systematic humiliation by staff of boys who were 'no good at sport.' The cane (6) was widely applied. All four of my 'swishings' were for uncommitted offences and I do not accept that 'it did not do me any harm.' It filled me with a sense of injustice and resentment and a desire for revenge.

The snobbery and class placing were all-pervasive. We were endlessly told how fortunate we were to be attending such a wonderful school at no cost to our parents. We had to wear our uniform caps on the school buses so that we would not be mistaken for the 'lesser beings' who went to the secondary modern school in the same street which had uniform of a similar colour, but without hats.

Occasionally we had sports fixtures with the local public schools, including the one that I might have attended as a 'poor scholarship boy.' The boys from these schools had a similar 'lesser beings' attitude to us using the term 'grammar schoolboy' as if it was the highest put-down and assertion of superiority imaginable. I dread to think what would have happened to me in such a place even though my mother desperately wanted me to go to the 'posh school' where the 'best people' sent their children. She never forgave my father for preventing it.

One of my few positive memories of unmitigated happiness from these years and also an opportunity to learn deeply satisfying skills was nothing to do with school but was another outcome of my mother's church cleaning. The local priest was quite a bit more enthusiastic about sailing than he was about God, in a conventionally devotional Anglican sense. Every Easter he would hire five or six four berth yachts on the Norfolk Broads. The crews were made up largely of the private preparatory and public-school boys of the parish, plus one or two privately educated girls, who were home for the holiday from their residential schools. Because of my mother's loyal but poorly paid cleaning of the church I was given a free place.

The vicar had a system for crewing the boats that I have come to totally approve of – and it had nothing to do with which school you went to. However old you were on your first trip you were a 'cabin boy or girl'. On the second trip, assuming you had not drowned on the first as he was no enthusiast for health and safety, you became a second mate. Next trip you were first mate and fourth trip a skipper. Most participants started these trips when they were about eleven or twelve so by fifteen it was perfectly possible to become a skipper, and I did.

With hindsight I guess you would have to say that he was irresponsible. There were no life jackets, though in theory being able to swim was required, and no roll calls. Each boat would have a small lugsail clinker built sailing dinghy in tow and the younger crew were encouraged to learn about the wind by messing about in them when the fleet was at anchor. When I was about ten years-old I sailed out of sight of the main fleet when it stopped for lunch. I loved to lie in the bottom of the dinghy and be hypnotised by the 'fluff, fluff, fluff, fluff' sound of the blunt bow churning through the wavelets of the river or broad.

When I returned to the lunchtime anchorage, I found that the fleet had upped anchor and gone. It took me an hour of frantic rowing and sailing to catch up with them and no-one had even noticed that I was missing. I did not tell my mother! On reflection the system whereby authority depended on competence rather than age or class was a very interesting one, which I was to make use of a lot as a teacher. Years later when I visited Sudbury Valley School in Framingham, Massachusetts I found such a competence-based system being used to run the various 'corporations' or departments of the school (Greenberg 1992).

In England Labour party 'limited idealism' has largely abolished the grammar schools and the iniquitous 11+ test but has never had the courage or political will to tackle the expensive private 'public schools' even to the extent of challenging their charitable tax status which allows them to avoid paying VAT. Yet historically they have been stolen from the poor. Now the Conservatives hold them up as models of excellence to be preserved at all costs. The state system is told that it has to be 'driven up' to these academic heights by a regime of tests and inspections. No mention of cost of course, or small classes, or beautiful environments, or of the social divisions and peer networking that the elite schools so carefully cultivate. In the third decade of the twenty-first century we British are once again being ruled by their products while the gulf between rich and poor widens.

At the same time data is becoming available that shows beyond doubt that where there are grotesque and growing gaps between the wealth of rich and poor it is less and less possible to live in a healthy, peaceful, low crime and democratic society (Wilkinson and Pickett, 2010).

Poverty is not just bad for the poor. It is bad for everyone. We also know from the OECD PISA (OECD, 2009) studies that the academic achievement of the students at the private fee-paying schools is no better than would be expected given the social privilege and advantage of their home backgrounds. The 'excellence' claim is a big lie. Even the claim (Acemoglu et.al., 2012) that social equality hinders innovation and that inequality appears to correlate with higher levels of economic innovation has recently been discredited by the work of Hopkin, Lapuente and Moller (2014) who demonstrate that more equal and 'cuddly capitalist' Sweden and Switzerland have higher levels of patent applications per head than the massively less equal 'cutthroat capitalist' United States. There is no necessary 'trade-off' between equality and innovation. In fact, all the work of Ricardo Semler at Semco suggests exactly the opposite (Semler 1988, 2003).

I left grammar school with six O-levels (7) and a deep learned hostility towards the English class system. It was not just a quaint and benign 'Downton Abbeyesque' 'rich man in his castle, poor man at the gate' structure in which all could feel a sense of identity and belonging. This mask quickly fell away if it was questioned. On the contrary when challenged it showed itself to be a malignant power network that would unhesitatingly mock and diminish questioning from 'below.'

I also vividly remember asking how it was possible for a school system claiming to be educational to totally disregard my interests and experiences and give me absolutely no help whatever in understanding either myself or how to live a worthwhile life. I knew then that I was interested in many things and that had school tapped into my motivation the sky would have been the limit as far as learning was concerned. As to careers advice there was none. If you were not 'staying on' as a potential university candidate the school could not have been less interested in you. The pleasure of burning our caps on the last day of school was intense! It encapsulated the waste of it all as far as I was concerned.

Chapter 2 – Work

My first job as a general clerical officer at the London County Council met many of my father's criteria for 'getting on.' I worked indoors in an office that, although very small, had a carpet on the floor and I was paid a monthly salary, much to my annoyance. My friends in manual work got paid weekly wages which seemed to make them perpetually more 'flush' with cash than me. The job made only the most modest demands on my understanding of calculus or book one of Xenophon's Hellenica.

Tucked away in an upstairs nook of Admiralty Arch, just off Trafalgar Square with a view of Buckingham Palace, it involved opening the morning post from the head park keepers of London's forty-seven parks requesting a resupply of certain posters.

There were 423 different posters from 'Dogs must not urinate on the grass' to 'Model aircraft may be flewn (unique London Parks spelling!) between 2pm and 3.30pm on alternate WEDNESDAYS' – or something similar. I had to put the required quantity of the required poster into a tube and place it in the 'out tray' which was emptied twice a day by Paddy, an ex-Grenadier Guards Irish messenger, who took them to the post room.

The upside of the job was that it took about two and a half hours per day to do it so by eleven-thirty I was listening to jazz records in Doug Dobell's record shop in the Charing Cross Road. At around three o'clock I would wander back to my cubby-hole of an 'office.' I would then walk slowly past the glass door of my boss' office three floors below, holding any piece of paper to hand to let him know that I was in the building and very busy. Then to the post-room to have a cup of tea with Paddy, listen once again to his story of being blown up in the King David Hotel during active service in Palestine, out by the back stairs and most days be on the four fifteen fast train to Orpington, my home town, from Charing Cross station.

After a few months of this joke of a job I met a draughtsman from the 'park design' department in the toilet one day. He played the drums and he invited me to join him on piano playing lunch-time gigs in pubs along the Old Kent Road. This fitted nicely into both our extended lunch 'hours' and provided a bit of ready cash.

One day when I was bemoaning the utter tedium of my 'work' and its failure so far to help me 'get on' he told me that there was an advertisement in his office for trainee valuation surveyors. I applied, on the basis that it could not be more boring than my present post, and was successful. With hindsight I can see that it was an excellent five-year professional training scheme if you were interested in valuing, buying or managing property. Unfortunately, I was not.

One day per week at Brixton School of Building prepared us for the examinations of the Royal Institute of Chartered Surveyors. These were very easy though a bit more challenging than putting posters in tubes. Some of the characters that I worked with were memorable like the brilliant Jewish surveyor who was also the communist mayor of a London borough whose greatest pleasure in life was buying slums for only their site value from mostly Jewish landlords. By the time demolition costs had been deducted from the purchase price the rogue landlords often got nothing at all for their property. 'We Jews invented ethics,' he would say, 'and these exploiters of the poor should be ashamed of themselves.' I learned more about the problems of the Middle East from Paddy and Manny than I had at school!

I was also learning a lot about the social conditions of the East End of London and how not to care for communities. When streets of technically 'unfit for human habitation' houses were demolished the communities would be destroyed. Old people would be moved to specialist housing, young families would be moved away to 'out county' estates, single people would be moved to maisonettes in different parts of London. As a result, the web of relationships that nurtured the children would be broken. The realisation of the importance of organic community for the well-being of human beings has never left me and eventually impelled me as a secondary school vice-principal to become an active member of the community school movement.

Having moved over the River Thames from Admiralty Arch to New County Hall on the South Bank it was no longer easy to get to the jazz record shops in Charing Cross Road at lunch time - however much I extended it. I found two other interesting places to visit instead that did not have to wait for lunch. One was an amazing circular library in County Hall known as the 'member's library' which existed mainly for the exclusive use of elected councillors though London teachers were also allowed access. It never seemed to have anyone in it except an occasional teacher.

Starting from my school knowledge of Xenophon I discovered that he had been a contemporary of a man called Socrates who did something called philosophy. (How could I have studied Ancient Greek for three years at school and not know this!?) This struck me as being particularly interesting for a person like myself who was fairly desperately trying to find some meaning in life.

The philosophy section of the library was well stocked and untouched by 'members' as far as I could see. I was not permitted to join the library so using a carrier bag instead of a membership ticket I worked my way steadily from Anaximander to Zeno. It did not feel like stealing as I always brought the books back when I had read them, though getting them back was sometimes riskier than 'borrowing' them in the first place.

I had realised by this time that many reasonably intelligent people of my age were at places called 'universities' so I decided to award myself a degree in philosophy. I used a well-worn second hand copy of Bertrand Russell's 'History of Western Philosophy' (1946) as my tutor, bought from a bookstall in the Cut market at the back of Waterloo Station. I was very pleased to award myself a first-class degree in philosophy with a special distinction in the pre-Socratics though I wished that Bertrand Russell had been a real-life tutor to help me with the hard bits rather than just living in a book. (Strangely I was to get to know him a little only a year or two later). Even so it was a wonderful experience, and another classic example of how much can be learned when motivated by real interest even though in my heart I began to wish that I was a real student at a real university.

I read philosophy books everywhere and spent longer and longer in what felt like my private library. I learned that I could walk out of whatever office I was temporarily attached to as a trainee at any time I chose so long as I looked as if I was doing something important and carried sufficiently prominent pieces of paper. I remember struggling for a long time with Heidegger in boring mathematics classes at Brixton School of Building and still getting 100% in the end of year mensuration test. In fact, part-time study for surveying examinations became very part time indeed.

The other perk of my trainee surveyor years was the discovery of another unused source of pleasure in County Hall. This was the member's reading room. Once again unused by members so far as I could see it contained several fresh daily newspapers each day and, even better, an excellent grand piano in perfect tune.

A trainee architect friend from what was then British Guiana used to bring his bongo drums to work most days and we would play jazz standards through many lunch hours as a duo. We were probably doing the piano a favour as all good quality musical instruments like to be played. We both agreed that it was very imaginative of the London County Council to provide such creative occupational therapy facilities for its overworked and highly stressed trainees.

Occasionally other trainee surveyors, engineers and architects would come to listen unless I had a gig in an Old Kent Road pub with my draughtsman friend from the Parks Department. On those days he would pick me up in an official car pool Ford Popular for the five-minute journey South. Whereabouts in his office he hid his drum kit I never found out!

All this and I still managed to be on an early train to Orpington – still the 16.15 fast from Charing Cross more often than not, though when I got on it had become the 16.18 from Waterloo East. Sometimes my musical mentor Bert Barnes would be on this train. I used to talk to him about some of the philosophy books I was reading. He always listened and made his own suggestions.

Once, when I was working through the Existentialists, I told him about a confused and confusing book that I was reading called 'The Outsider' by Colin Wilson. I had mistakenly acquired it when looking for Camus' book of the same title. 'If you find that interesting try 'The Moon and Sixpence' by Somerset Maugham,' suggested Bert. I did and found it spellbinding. Then he suggested Aldous Huxley. It opened up the whole field of Eastern religions with their emphasis on non-attachment and inner quietness. As well as talking about books we talked a lot about politics. He had some pretty strong views about the importance of trade unions and of democracy itself. He worked for one of the then many print unions – NATSOPA I think. I never found out what the letters stood for.

As a teenager Bert had grown up in Camberwell, a very poor part of South London, and had belonged to a Methodist youth club called Clubland in the Walworth Road. It had left an indelible mark on him. The club was run by an eccentric minister called the Rev James Butterworth (1933). As well as normal youth club activities, which included a club dance band, there was a club parliament where all significant club decisions were made. Every member of the club of whatever age was a member of the Clubland parliament which met in the church itself with each member having his or her own parliamentary pew. The member who was the elected 'speaker' sat in the minister's seat and conducted business along the lines of the House of Commons.

'Butterworth had two aims,' explained Bert. 'Firstly, to teach kids about democracy by doing it.' He wanted the members to learn to be responsible through having responsibility in order to stop them being drawn into any of the criminal activities to which this poor part of South London was prone. Butterworth's second aim was to develop a strong and responsible loyalty to the club. It made a powerful lifelong impression on Bert who attributed his whole philosophy of life to the quality of the Clubland experience. It had a similar effect on another member, the actor Michael Caine, who featured

Butterworth in a 1969 television film about his formative experiences.

Clubland parliamentary life had its humorous side. Apparently, the local Methodist equivalent of a bishop strongly disapproved of Butterworth's methods and would try to catch him using the church for inappropriate purposes. To guard against this a club member would be posted outside the church whenever the parliament was sitting. If an unwelcome visitation was made by higher authority a signal would be given and the whole parliament would pick up hymn books and begin to sing! I remember thinking that it would be a good idea if schools had parliaments never dreaming that thirty years later I would be travelling the world visiting schools that had!

After passing my surveyors examinations and beginning to earn a professional salary I realised that I was 'getting on' but not enjoying it very much. So I took a large pay cut and went to work for OXFAM instead as an assistant area organiser. This was more like it! Interesting, varied, worthwhile in my eyes, and given a great deal of freedom to organise my own working life. One of the most enjoyable parts of my new job was visiting schools and talking with older students about the problems facing the under-developed and developing parts of the world. Exploring the issues with intelligent and idealistic young people was exciting. Even more exciting to me was that I was good at it. The students often became highly motivated fund raisers and the schools regularly invited me back.

At around this time I met the person who was to become my wife. She came to shake a tin at a street collection that I was organizing in Oxford. When it started to rain, she decided that it would be drier to talk to me instead. Marriage looked like becoming a reality and I realised that in order to answer my future father-in-law's question 'will you be able to maintain property?' I needed a 'proper' job that would enable me to buy a house - in order to be able to maintain it!

Oxfam did not pay professional wages in the early nineteen sixties so what to do? Asking myself what had I most enjoyed doing in the previous few years up came the answer 'working with older school students.' So, I decided to become a teacher. But – I had no A levels let alone a degree. I discovered that as I was a little older than most applicants, I could get a place at a college of education just outside Oxford with just my memories of calculus and Xenophon if I agreed to study for some A levels by correspondence course. I tried Music and History, passed them both after six months, and took up my place as a trainee junior/secondary teacher specialising in these two subjects.

I really need to say a little about my musical education prior to studying for the A level as it is pertinent to my belief in pupil choice and how to develop, or not develop, innate talent. When I was ten years old my mother had acquired a piano from a local green grocer. I remember it being delivered in his van which knocked it permanently much more out of tune than it already was. I was thrilled and immediately began to pick out tunes from the Billy Cotton Bandshow that I heard on the radio.

My mother found a music teacher who taught a good friend of mine from school. With some reluctance I began to work for Grade One of the Associated Board examinations. Distinction. Teacher was very pleased with me. I was then entered straight for Grade Four which again I passed with distinction though I was beginning to get seriously fed up about not being consulted – even as to which pieces to prepare from the choice offered. I had to play the pieces that the teacher preferred, or perhaps found easiest to teach and for which I would get the highest grade.

My teacher also began to enter me for competitive music festivals without consulting me. This made me very angry and determinedly subversive. I just could not see the point of trying to play a movement of a Mozart piano sonata 'better' than anyone else in front of a lot of cold fish judges just for the greater glory of my music teacher. After two of these highly unfestive 'festivals' I told my mother I would not do it anymore.

By this time, after two years of lessons, I was getting quite good at playing Billy Cotton Bandshow tunes not just with my right hand for the melody but with rudimentary left-hand accompaniments as well. One day waiting for my lesson I began to play 'Twenty Tiny Fingers' on my teacher's Bechstein expecting her to be impressed. She was horrified. She shouted 'don't ever play that rubbish on my beautiful piano!' That was it. You don't like my music and I don't like yours. That evening I 'lost' my music case in a snowdrift at the bus stop on my way home. My mother could not afford to replace it or the music so my 'official' music lessons with an 'official' teacher stopped there and then.

Fortunately, another much more sympathetic music teacher was shortly to appear in my life. My best friend's father, the same Bert Barnes that I was later to talk to on the train about politics, democratic communities for young people and philosophy, had been a professional jazz guitarist in the army during the second world war. He had played in an outfit with English comedian Charlie Chester called the 'Stars in Battledress.'

One day I was picking out a new Billy Cotton tune on the Barnes' new piano and struggling to provide an accompaniment. Bert sat down beside me and said 'I like the right hand but why don't you try working out some proper chords for the left hand.' I knew a little about chords from Grade Four theory but had no idea how to apply them. He showed me. Soon we were playing 'Sunny Side of the Street', 'Ain't Misbehavin' ', 'I Can't Give You Anything But Love' on guitar and piano.

My friend Dave and I would alternate right and left-hand parts while Bert supported us with his punchy swinging guitar. Sometimes Dave played guitar and Bert would become Stephane Grappelli on violin. Heaven had opened. I was learning to be a jazz player and far from being nagged by my mother to 'do your practice', which had meant fooling her with the same easy piece every time or the same scale in C major, nothing could now stop me from playing. I practised for hours learning new tune after new tune, moving to more and more complex chords and styles, listening to every jazz pianist I could find. Earl Hines, Fats Waller, Teddy Wilson, Erroll Garner, Count Basie, Oscar Peterson, Art Tatum, Bud Powell and then by the late fifties the great bebop pianists and avant-gardists like Horace Silver, Wynton Kelly and Thelonius Monk.

Dave and I began to get paid gigs when we were still teenagers where our speciality was to switch instruments in the middle of a tune. When he was on piano I would play drums and when I was on piano he would move to the drum-kit. We were well underage when we started gigging at pubs, river boats on the Thames, in the Arches bars on Brighton sea-front and anywhere else that would have us.

The lesson I draw from this is that if only my original music teacher had valued what I was struggling to do for myself and encouraged me in the way that Bert Barnes did I would have happily played her Mozart in return and would probably have learned to love his beautiful music much sooner than I did. Once again, I was asking 'why does no-one listen to the learners and encourage their interests?'

Strangely, my jazz playing was crucial in gaining admittance to the teacher's course for music. A course entry requirement as well as A level music was grade eight performance standard on voice or instrument. I did not have either of these but the lecturer handling the admissions that year happened to be a Karl Orff enthusiast who wanted to develop a new improvised music course for use in schools. She spotted my jazz background on my application letter and decided to interview me.

It was wonderful. The interview consisted of moving around a music room playing 'shouts and responses' to each other on a wide range of instruments with more emphasis on imagination than technical competence. Sixty-year-old apparently very conventional music teacher and twenty-four-year-old jazz musician exploring sound together. She muttering 'yes' after an especially good bit and me muttering 'yeah'. It was straight out of Hollywood! I was in my element and ended up more or less leading this part of the course for her after she won a vigorous argument with her head of department over whether to admit me.

One of the more difficult tasks was to help other students who had obediently worked through their grades to dare to improvise and risk playing 'wrong' notes. This can be very difficult and sometimes impossible. I think the head of department was slightly annoyed when three years later I was awarded the highest mark of the year in the final examinations and he had to present me with a prize. He chose the published version of his doctoral thesis on an obscure Beethoven piano sonata. I imagine he thought I would find it unreadable though actually by this time I was coming to appreciate classical music and so rather enjoyed it.

While working for the A levels by correspondence course I had to find a job in Oxford that paid a bit more than the pittance I had earned with OXFAM. I found a job as a nursing assistant in a therapeutic community in a large psychiatric hospital.

This also proved to be very interesting and very pertinent to my future career. The unit consisted of seventy or so patients, suffering from a range of conditions, most of whom were below the age of thirty-five. There was a full complement of nurses, psychiatrists, occupational therapists and a psychologist. Treatment consisted basically of the experience of living together in a community.

The community life was built around two daily democratic community meetings at which many of the day to day decisions affecting the management of the unit were made and many questions were asked about the behaviour of both patients and staff. All members of the community, staff and patients, were known by their first names from most senior consultant to newest admission, no uniforms were worn and as little medication as possible was prescribed. (Coincidentally there were also carpets on the floor unlike other parts of the hospital – 'Christian names and carpets' once again!) After every community meeting there would be an extended staff meeting where progress, medication changes, and possible discharges were discussed along with the inner states of individual staff members many of whom found the work very personally demanding at times.

Some of my funniest memories are of visits by medical students with their white coats and stethoscopes from Oxford university medical school who would say 'this is madness! We can't tell who are staff and who are patients.' Lars von Trier could have made his own version of 'One Flew Over the Cuckoo's Nest' from some of the happenings! The most hilarious incident during my eight months on the unit was when a patient called Ernie decided to 'liberate' a visiting medical student's white coat and stand in the middle of the Oxford to Reading main road directing all the rush hour traffic into the hospital grounds – including a police traffic car. The chaos was indescribable. He explained that the coat had 'a nice air of authority' about it and as he had never had any authority in his life as a farm labourer he wanted to see what it was like.

While I was there, I had the opportunity to work with the unit psychologist on a statistical study of the effectiveness of the democratic community therapy. The measure for success was readmission rate and the relative damage done by the side effects of medication and electro-convulsive therapy (ECT) that was used widely in the rest of the hospital but never in our unit. The findings were very interesting. Re-admission rates for our unit were exactly the same as readmission rates for similar patients with comparable conditions in normal psychiatric hospitals using physical treatments. However due to the low usage of medication and total absence of ECT the side effects that patients had to live with were virtually nil.

So, although they had to return to hospital just as often as other patients their minds were much more 'their own', their memories much more intact, and their feelings much more available to them than would otherwise have been the case. The research fascinated me as it raised many questions about 'what does it mean to be human?' - familiar from my philosophical and now psychological reading.

Working on the unit was a powerful hands-on introduction to the use of a democratic meeting as a tool for learning which resonated strongly with all that Bert Barnes had told me about Clubland. In the case of the unit this involved learning how to understand and manage one's own difficulties and to care for and support others who were doing the same, whether one was staff or patient.

I began to feel that much of this could be transferred to schools with the bonus of learning how to manage a democratic mini-society in the school as an educational preparation for being an adult in wider democratic society, just as Butterworth had done at Clubland. Therapy and Education would coalesce along a seamless continuum of learning as personal need and the capacity to manage one's difficulties became united in a broader social understanding, thus enabling the personal contribution to society of an effective citizen. If it was possible to have a minimally coercive psychiatric unit for young people why could we not have minimally or even non-coercive schools? Surely coercion did not enable real learning to happen I thought, looking back on my own schooling? Surely what was needed was the motivation generated by curiosity and interest in a collaborative democratic community?

There was much talk about the value of democracy and freedom at this time as it was the height of the cold war and our leaders said that they were prepared to destroy the world in nuclear war for the sake of it! The Cuban missile crisis had taken the world to the edge of mutually assured destruction. The whole idea of nuclear war and the preparations for it seemed utterly crazy to me and I became quite involved in the anti-nuclear movement. Almost by accident, attending a meeting on behalf of somebody else, I became a member of the anti-nuclear Committee of 100 for a while.

As well as meeting some extraordinary people such as Vanessa Redgrave, Robert Bolt and John Osborne I finally met my philosophical 'tutor' Bertrand Russell in the flesh. Though very old and very tired he had a good chuckle about the idea of a trainee surveyor using one of his books as a guide to reading all the otherwise unread philosophy books in the London County Council members' library. He pointedly told me that I would have had to handle the existentialists on my own as he detested them all from Kierkegaard to Sartre and had ignored them in his History of Western Philosophy! He didn't tell me that he had once founded a democratic school – Beacon Hill. I discovered that much later.

The experience on the community therapy unit proved to be another piece of serendipity that formed my thinking about education and exactly what kind of teacher I wanted to become. At this stage I had never heard of A.S. Neill, Homer Lane, Bertrand Russell himself, and all the other innovators who used democratic meetings in their schools. I was soon to discover these in another unused part of another library.

Chapter 3 – Training to be a Teacher

The three years as a student preparing for a junior/secondary teacher's certificate proved to be rather tedious and undemanding with the glorious exception of the music improvisation and composition workshops and two of the three teaching practices in schools.

All my fears of and detestation for compulsory physical education from school returned and so I put my newly purchased and unworn track suit in my locker on the first day of the three-year course and left it there. It might still be there for all I know as I just did not attend physical education sessions. As a non-resident mature student nobody ever seemed to notice my absence which suited me fine and I was duly awarded a pass for physical education on my teacher's certificate after three years of non-attendance.

Psychology lectures also presented problems as the lecturer was an enthusiastic behaviourist. Or at least he thought he was. I have since learned that there is much more to Skinner and even Pavlov than the simplistic justification for the 'behaviour management' of children advocated by this lecturer. Having just come from the subtleties and complexities of the ideas of Freud, Anna Freud, Jung, Klein, Erikson, Bowlby, Laing and Winnicott, which provided the theoretical underpinning to the psychiatric therapeutic community where I had previously worked, I could not see quite what Pavlov's salivating dogs (Babkin, 1949) and Skinner's rats pulling levers in boxes (Skinner, 1968) had to do with the education of children and young people!

I was more interested in ideas that would help to create a classroom that served as a 'holding environment' within which learners could become their 'true selves' with all the release of energy, curiosity, collaboration, spontaneity, motivation to learn that that would entail. In my view this behaviourist 'behaviour management' approach was all about producing the easily manipulated and controlled 'false selves' that Winnicott describes with all the associated tendencies to emptiness, depression, loss of self-esteem and lack of empathy that follows (1971, 1973). Perfect material for an exploitative capitalism about which I would later learn that Freire (1974) and Habermas (1962 and 1989) would have a lot to say. This was definitely not what I wanted to do to young people.

My objective when I became a teacher was exactly what Habermas describes as the 'revival of the public sphere' in a direct democracy in a classroom based as much as was legally and institutionally possible on the equal rights and responsibilities of the citizens of the class community. I intended as much as possible to be a just another citizen though accepting that there would be times when I would have to be primus inter pares if I wanted to keep my job.

I became a persistent and probably highly irritating asker of subversive questions which tended and were intended to throw the lecturers off their stride. This also annoyed the other students who just wanted to take reams of verbatim notes to reproduce in the examination. In a private discussion the psychology lecturer and I did a deal. We agreed that as a mature student with some psychological experience I could create my own psychology course based on reading in the library instead of attending his lectures. I would set my own essay and examination questions subject to his prior approval.

Looking back on it I can't quite believe that this actually happened and that I got away with it. But it presented an amazing opportunity. I discovered not only the books by Jerome Bruner (with whom I was later to work when I was head of the humanities department in a very large comprehensive school near Oxford and he was a visiting professor at the university), but also, in a dusty and unvisited part of the library, a shelf full of all the books by A.S. Neill. These were as unread as the philosophy books had been in the County Hall member's library!

And not just Neill but Homer Lane, W.B. Curry, J.H. Simpson, Kees Boeke, David Wills, Bertrand and Dora Russell, Tolstoy, Dewey all of whom spoke of the importance of respecting and trusting children as people with full rights as human beings. Children were to be treated not as rats or dogs, to be manipulated and motivated by marks and grades, but as human beings worthy of respect, whose interests and passions were to be valued, nurtured and encouraged. Above all they were to be given the opportunity to participate freely in democratic decision making and to create and manage for themselves appropriate democratic structures and processes. This made absolute sense and fitted perfectly with what I had learned about Clubland and from working in the therapeutic community.

I made profuse notes from these books which I used as the basis for my final B.Ed. extended essay which bore the somewhat ponderous title of 'A Study of the work of Homer Lane and its influence on Three English Educators – W. David Wills, A.S. Neill, and J.H. Simpson, with particular reference to their use of Various Forms of Shared Responsibility or Self-Government.' I identified strongly with Lane's belief (1928) that the essential quality for young people to have as people was self-respect, which almost without exception would develop from the experience of being respected themselves by trusted adult role models. Some young people would get this from their families but many would not. I felt that at last, and belatedly, I was beginning to find such people in my own life. They had been missing from my family and school experiences. I warmed to Lane's belief that self-respect would grow in partnership with self-reliance given the right opportunities.

Sharing in the decision making in a democratic school or institution community would slowly allow the quality of self-restraint to emerge as the young people realised that they actually shared personally the responsibility for the maintenance of order and well-being of others in the community. Even then this seemed to me to represent the core requirement for being a citizen of a democratic society. Even though some families, though by no means all, would help young people to develop self-respect and even self-reliance schools had a responsibility to develop those qualities in a wider setting than the family where the need for self-restraint could be learned in preparation for adulthood.

I began to realise that this was even more important than the academic learning which seemed to be the main concern of schools, and then only for the more successful. It seemed almost ironic to realise that in fact these qualities, well understood by Maslow (1954) and Bruner (1966) and Vygotsky (Holzman and Newman 1993), but apparently little valued by the schools that I had attended, were also essential for purposeful, meaningful and deep academic study. Even though I fairly quickly forgot that I had written this essay in reality it has underpinned all the educational work that I have done ever since.

Fortunately, I discovered this goldmine of literature shortly before my first teaching practice. It was my good luck to arrive in the nondescript and drab red brick primary school on a council estate to the south of Oxford city just as the top junior class teacher became seriously ill. The head teacher welcomed me with open arms and for six weeks I was allowed to do much as I liked so long as the he received no complaints from parents or other teachers. There was no 11+ examination to prepare for as the children would all be going to the same secondary school without selection. By this time Oxford had largely closed its selective grammar schools and switched to a comprehensive school system - and, of course, there was no prescribed national curriculum at this time. Heaven!

On my first morning I got to the classroom before the children and put all the desks to one side and set out all the chairs in a circle. The puzzled children arrived and all found seats eventually. I explained that I was going to be their teacher for the next six weeks and that we were going to decide together what we would study and how we would manage the class, apart from some arithmetic lessons which the head teacher required me to teach, and a period for private reading every day which was the policy of the whole school. I also explained that at some point I hoped the children would teach their topics to the rest of the class. A list of topics quickly emerged, one of which was 'the Ancient Egyptians' which had already been part of the previous class teacher's curriculum.

The class then got into groups to talk about their shared interests and plan what they would do. Topics ranged from 'Football', 'fashion', 'pop music', 'fishing' and 'dinosaurs' to the 'Battle of Britain.' Resources for most of the topics were minimal on the shelves of the classroom so a representative from each group scoured the rudimentary school library for anything useful. Children also agreed to bring materials from home, though I feared that in many cases that would not produce much in terms of books, though perhaps some artefacts would emerge.

I was right about the books but the big surprise was that it eventually produced something else even more useful that I had not expected at all – mums and dads and grandparents. For my part after school I went straight to the quite well stocked college resource centre for teaching materials and filled my van with stuff. The tables were arranged in groups depending on the number of children working on each topic. Several children ended up working on their own which gradually came to worry me as it became clear that they were isolated not just by their unusual choice of topic but also by their personalities and, in two cases, by the fact that other children disliked them.

I was required by the college to prepare my lessons minute by minute. This of course was impossible but I did keep a detailed diary of everything that happened. I was extremely fortunate in the supervising tutor who was allocated to me. Just by chance he was the college tutor in the 'philosophy of education.' Although his lectures were not very exciting he was so pleased to have a student who had actually read philosophy books from choice and who had heard of Rousseau and Dewey that we became good friends.

His first visit found a fairly chaotic classroom with children engaged in a very wide range of activities. The most spectacular activity was the re-enactment of the 1940 air Battle of Britain. This involved flying homemade cardboard and balsa wood Spitfires and Hurricanes against cardboard Junkers 88s suspended by threads of cotton from the ceiling. My tutor loved it and once he had read my diary never once asked for lesson plans. We had some good discussions about what the children were doing. I was concerned about the amount of copying and tracing that was going on. Some children would happily do it for hours. We called a class meeting to discuss this and two very important developments emerged.

The first was that as well as just collecting 'stuff' around their topics and producing posters and displays consisting of copied pictures and pieces of writing the children would be encouraged and expected to ask questions. They would then organise their work around these questions such as 'why did dinosaurs die out' or 'why do human beings wear clothes' or 'why did we win the Battle of Britain?' This gave the presentations a keener sense of purpose by introducing an element of research and a higher order of thinking. Although this seems totally obvious the idea that children should approach their studies from the perspective of asking and answering their own questions had never been mentioned at the college.

The second development that emerged from the class meeting was quite different but also very important for the remaining weeks of the teaching practice. One girl said that her mother specialised in making 'old fashioned wedding dresses' and could she come to the class to talk about her work and show the students' 'fashion' group some of her products. Some of the boys objected until it emerged that one of the dads of the group studying football was a coach and qualified referee. We agreed to invite him as well.

Fortunately, my tutor reminded me to clear the idea with the head teacher who was delighted to get a bit of interest in the school from parents and enthusiastically agreed.

The visits and talks by parents were immensely popular with the children. Over the coming weeks we had contributions from grandparents as well, one of whom had been a member of the Royal Observer Corps in London during the bombing blitz that followed the Battle of Britain. It was my first experience of the idea that learning could involve the family and the wider community. Some of the groups ran out of ideas before the six weeks were up so they presented their topic to the rest of the class when they were ready and then moved on to something else of their choice. Most did not present until the final week. Immense care went into the presentation 'lessons' and in several cases parents came back to listen. Motivation was sky high.

The head teacher was delighted and my tutor assessed my work as 'excellent' even though most of it had been made up as I went along. (Interesting that this should much later become the title of the book about Albany Free School written by the very inspiring teacher and educator Chris Mercogliano – 'Making it up as we go along – The Story of Albany Free School.' (1998)).

In contrast to this my second teaching practice a year later in the history department of a local comprehensive secondary school was a disaster. At first the head of department insisted on tightly prepared lessons for the different work being done by the first, second, and third year classes that I was allowed to teach. He would sit at the back of the class and comment if he felt that I had not made a point clearly enough. Some of the pupils did not like him much and took their feelings out on me. The question of discipline and anti-teacher behaviour had just not arisen on my first practice so this was a bit of a shock.

After the first two weeks he began to stay in the staffroom, which suited me as I could use part of a lesson to discuss with the classes just how they felt about history. The first complaint was usually about the boring and unattractive nature of the text-books being used, which was true, and the second was about the teacher who 'never listens to our ideas.' One of these discussions was joined by my college tutor who had the sense to warn me about allowing the students to discuss their feelings towards their regular teacher. It was too late however. Somehow it had got back to him and I received a warning about 'unprofessional behaviour'.

Both the third-year classes that I taught were studying 'transport in the industrial revolution.' Here was an opportunity, I thought, to try the group research project method I had used in the primary school. I made a list of possible topics such as 'the growth of the turnpikes', 'the rise and fall of the canals', 'the coming of the railways' all of which were topics that I was supposed to cover in two or three lessons. I thought the students would be more motivated and get involved at greater depth if they prepared a topic in groups and presented it to the whole class with me as back-up if they said things that were hopelessly inaccurate. The classes were enthusiastic and got to work.

My mistake, often repeated throughout my teaching career, was not to have consulted higher authority. The head of department somehow heard about what I was doing and insisted on observing one of the student taught lessons. He sat at the back and succeeded in undermining the confidence of the students in making their presentation, and me in trying to support them. It was a bad experience for all concerned. My tutor told me to put up with it, keep my head down and survive the remaining weeks. Out of respect for him I did, though if he had sided with the head of department, I think my teaching career would have ended then and there. I was given a grudging 'satisfactory only' by the school with the comment that 'Mr Hannam should understand that as a student teacher he should not conduct inappropriate experiments in class democracy.' My tutor managed to fudge all this with some ameliorating comments about 'difficult circumstances.' It looked as if my future lay in primary and not secondary schools!

The third teaching practice provided another contrast. This time I was put into another top year primary class whose teacher was an ex-army officer who was about to retire. If he was not an alcoholic then he was certainly fond of a drink or two, and not just in the evenings. He loved two things in life; having fun with children and sailing and probably not in that order.

As it was my final and most heavily assessed teaching practice, I was expected to take full responsibility for the class. That suited me fine. When I explained to the class teacher the sort of democratically negotiated pupil choice project work, built around children devising their own organising questions, that I had in mind I got a big surprise. Instead of saying 'maybe, but I will need to keep an eye on it' he just said 'Great. I've always wanted to try something like that! Let's do it together!' My heart sank as I talked it over with my tutor. I did not want the class teacher to be around. I had hoped that he would put his feet up in the staff room and leave me to get on with it. My tutor wisely said that really I had no choice but to give the team teaching approach a try, as if he argued with the head teacher on my behalf for my right to be in 'sole charge' it would not set a very good tone for the practice or be well received by the class teacher who would be involved in my assessment.

In reality my fears were groundless. The class teacher and I did it together and it was tremendous. Much better than if I had been alone. It was my first, but not my last, experience of team teaching. The school was in a much more middle-class area than that of my first teaching practice and the problem was not getting parents into the school but keeping them out! Almost every child wanted to bring someone in to talk about something they were doing or had done and the final project presentations had to use the school hall as we could not get everyone into the classroom. The head teacher came too and talked about his own childhood experiences with horses as part of the 'pony' topic group presentation. Another 'excellent' assessment confirmed my feelings about a career in primary schools.

I was just beginning to think about looking for jobs when a new opportunity appeared. The government decided to introduce the B.Ed., a bachelor's degree in Education. This enabled some student teachers at colleges of education to have the opportunity to study for a fourth year and upgrade their teacher's certificate to a full degree. Most universities willingly agreed to provide this extra year for their local colleges of education.

Things were not so simple at Oxford University of course and much debate ensued in the university governing senate as to whether they would offer this degree at all. Some powerful dons (professors and lecturers) did not want to touch it with a bargepole. They believed that no students worthy of an 'Oxon' degree could possibly come from a college of education and that inevitably standards would have to be lowered to accommodate them. Others said 'let's give it a try for one year' and they won the day. About twenty students, perhaps five per cent of the year group, were selected from the three colleges of education in the Oxford area to become the first B.Ed (Oxon) cohort.

The university, quite rightly in my opinion, had a pretty poor view of the quality of the academic teaching in the education colleges and insisted that the bachelor of education students become full members of the university with tutors from established Oxford colleges. Full access to the entire university lecture programme and libraries such as the Bodleian was given but the bar was raised very high with regard to the examinations required. Having won the music prize at the college I chose to make history my degree subject. This involved preparing for eight of the eleven 'history schools' papers that would be sat by the three-year university history undergraduates in just over eight months. This was a tough call but I loved the challenge, largely because it was self-chosen.

After being fairly bored by the low standards of the education college I found Oxford University academically amazing and exciting. For the first time in my life I felt I was learning at the depth and speed that my mind had cried out for many years and I was doing it because I wanted to. I did not need to be coerced. It was my choice. This despite the arrogant pomposity of many of the disproportionate number of overprivileged and 'entitled' public (elite private!) schoolboys who fill so many of the places at Oxford and Cambridge. As a married student with children I could take or leave the social side of the university and mostly I 'left' it apart from some good jazz.

The freedom to choose much of what you studied had the same motivating effect on me as it had on the primary school children during my teaching practices. There was a direct parallel. As long as you turned up with your essay at the weekly tutorial you could attend any lectures you liked on any subject that caught your interest. If this meant that you neglected the subject that you were supposed to be studying for your degree that was your responsibility and your problem.

At last I could go to philosophy lectures by my heroes A.J. Ayer and John Plamenatz in the flesh, as a real university student rather than as a self-taught reader in the London County Council member's library. My tutor was a very interesting American on secondment from Harvard who had helped President Kennedy set up the Peace Corps. On top of this I was in demand as a keyboard player and a drummer in several university jazz groups as well as playing in a regular Jimmy Smith inspired outfit started by a friend. We earned good money playing in the officer's clubs of nearby United States Air Force bases and classy Thameside hotels. Some of the people I played with were very talented, much more so than me, who went on to become quite famous as jazz musicians, though some of the most talented of these died of heroin overdoses. Even the married mature student grant was not too bad and now with two children and 'gig money' my wife Deborah and I were able to buy a small house of our own in nearby Littlemore.

I think that the Oxford university senate members who had feared dilution of standards in accepting students from the education colleges were proved wrong. One of their rather mean 'successes' had been an insistence that the B.Ed., although allowed the suffix 'Oxon', would not be classified into first, upper and lower second and third as were all other Oxford degrees. A special category of 'distinction' was created as recompense and several of us were awarded it. We had to go through the whole sub-fusc 'dressing up' absurdities of 'schools' but the bit of the examination that I recall as being most quintessentially 'Oxford' was my viva (oral). This was based on a question on Jeremy Bentham that I had answered in the political thought paper. I had compared him with Stalin I think and this so engaged the don conducting the examination that we massively overran the allocated twenty-minute time slot. He ended up inviting me to his college to continue the argument until he finally decided that he could award a mark. He told me at one point that either I was mad or very original indeed and he wanted to be sure which it was.

He never told me what he decided but I got my B.Ed. (Oxon) and later heard from my college of education tutor that the don had told him 'I've never had such a good argument in a viva before – and from a college of education candidate to boot! I had to re-examine my own view of Bentham and I've written books about the man!'

The old Etonians in the senate got their way however and, despite the success of the B.Ed. candidates, the university decided to scrap the degree after one year. More to do with snobbery than quality of candidate I felt, though it did give the degree a certain scarcity value as there are, and will only ever be, twenty-four of them!

I was now a qualified graduate teacher and set forth into the education system determined to see if I could get away with creating a responsibility sharing democratic learning.

PART TWO –

BECOMING A DEMOCRATIC TEACHER - PUTTING THE IDEAS INTO PRACTICE

Chapter 4 – My first job as a Teacher of Class 1H

My teaching practice experiences had made me sure that I did not want to work in the subject compartmentalised environment of a secondary school. The reality of finding a job forced me to think again. I saw an unusually worded advertisement for a 'humanities' teacher in a secondary modern school in a nearby county that retained selection at eleven. At this time in many counties and cities English eleven-year-old children in the state sector sat the 11+ examination that decided which ten to fifteen per cent or thereabouts would go to academic grammar schools. The remaining ninety per cent were 'selected' for vocational/practical courses in less well built, equipped and staffed secondary modern schools. There was supposed to be a third possibility of a dedicated and purpose built 'technical school' under the 'tri-partite system' created by the 1944 Education Act but in most parts of the country these did not exist.

The job entailed working almost as a primary school teacher with a class of eleven-year-olds. I would be both their form teacher and their teacher for English, History, Geography, Social Studies and Religious Education. This amounted to more than half their school week, timetabled as whole mornings or whole afternoons rather than isolated single periods. All seven first year classes were timetabled at the same time in one long corridor of adjacent rooms. There was a timetabled planning period with the intention that all the humanities teachers could meet and plan collaboratively.

The rest of the job involved teaching history to other years including ordinary and even advanced level GCE (General Certificate of Education) as this school was developing its own academic sixth form for sixteen to eighteen-year-olds, unusual for schools of this type. The school was in a more privileged part of the county town but even so only about ten to fifteen per cent of primary pupils were 'selected' for the local grammar schools. This meant that there were a good number of middle class '11+ failures' in the school.

I was interviewed by the head teacher as the head of the history department was away. This was fortunate for me as he was keen on all kinds of innovation and seemed to enjoy my descriptions of my primary teaching practice experiments. I was very interested in his description of the damaging effect that 'failing the 11+' had on the students. This was worst for those from middle-class families whose parents had had high expectations which were now destroyed as, in their perception and largely in reality, the hoped-for route to university and a professional career was now closed to their children.

He seemed to like my ideas about the importance of student participation in democratic decision making and the introduction of some self-directed learning. He was less interested in its intrinsic merits but rather as a way to rebuild the students' self-esteem. He warned me that the heads of the subject departments responsible for the various parts of the curriculum that I would teach were not too happy about the creation of 'humanities' taught by non-specialist teachers. He wanted to help the first-year students get used to secondary school through an introductory experience that offered a bridge from the primary school experience of being taught by just one teacher. He warned me that the heads of departments would try to compel me and the other six first year humanities teachers, several of whom were also new appointments, to teach tightly prescribed material from their subject specialisms in discrete subject lessons. On the other hand, he emphasised that he would be happy to see new ideas developed that were more integrated – though his conception of what this might look like seemed rather vague.

He created a new post of head of lower school who was also to be one of the first-year humanities teachers and de facto team leader, and gave the team a weekly time-tabled planning period of 50 minutes. He appointed an experienced and lively geography teacher from a neighbouring school to this post who was able to act as an experienced and effective buffer between the subject department heads and the humanities team. It was left unclear as to where final responsibility lay for control over the content of the curriculum and the teaching methods to be employed by each teacher. Here lay my opportunity!

This somewhat imprecise division of responsibilities created problems later but gave me relative carte blanche with my own class. In this job and those that followed I was regularly confronted with one overwhelming question.

'How far and how fast is it appropriate and possible to go towards creating a democratic and responsibility sharing learning community of self-directed learners in my own class or area of responsibility without ensuring that colleagues outside my area of responsibility clearly understood what I was doing?'

I always believed that it ought to be possible to persuade them to understand it sufficiently so that they would be disposed to tolerate what I was doing and not obstruct or feel threatened by it, even if they were not inclined to join in. Working out how to do this has always been a real dilemma for me and it was acutely the case for a probationary teacher working with more experienced, some very much more experienced, colleagues. But I had the support of the head teacher and trusting that he would smooth out any difficulties I plunged in and hoped for the best.

The evolution of the democratic class of 1H (First Year 'Hannam' class) developed in two distinct but interconnected ways; the management of the class and the organisation of the curriculum.

Chapter 5 – An amazing piece of synchronicity

Having made a start with this part of the book an extraordinary thing happened. On my Facebook page there appeared a faintly familiar face though I was confused by the baldness. The message said -

'You may just remember me. I'm Andrew! You were my class teacher in 1969-71. I have often wondered what you were up to and where your career took you - I was aware of your innovative ideas even then and it comes as no surprise to see you continuing in this! I just wanted to say what an inspiration you were to your pupils back then - some of us have very fond memories and consider you to have been a defining figure for us. Every good wish for your retirement years.'

Synchronicity at work, though I was far from retired! I don't want any retirement years! It turned out that Andrew was still in touch with a number of other students from the class. We met at his house for dinner and had an amazing evening of reminiscences. I have rewritten the rest of this chapter in the light of their comments and observations and here are a couple of examples. I include them at this point to set the rest of the chapter in the context of student recollections. I am slightly embarrassed to quote them verbatim as it seems somewhat self-congratulatory to do so - but they are a record of what can remain even after the passing of nearly 50 years. I regard them as a testament to the kind of relationships that are possible in an open and democratic classroom that might just encourage young teachers to give it a try, despite all the discouraging pressures that they are currently subjected to.

Andrew's memories – "I think we pupils were somewhat aware ourselves of the qualities we had as a group but I have always thought how lucky we were to engage with you... the combination was very special and I know some of our parents have commented over the years that you were the making of us! Maybe that works both ways!!

You once told my parents that I (at 12 years old) might go on to get geography degree - they told me later that at the time they thought it highly unlikely as eleven plus failures did not go to universities; my self-confidence wasn't high and I had never really shone at school up until then - but I did go to university and I did get a geography degree! Maybe that germ of an idea from you planted itself.

I don't recall much about the gathering of new entrants on their first day at The "G" Secondary Modern School. My family had moved to Aylesbury from Marlow a few weeks before the summer break and I had no group of friends to look out for. As the eldest of three I had no related experience of secondary life to draw on. I do recall my parents telling me that the school had a growing reputation as a forward-thinking school...maybe they believed it, maybe they were softening the pill of having 'failed' the 11 plus exam, possibly it was true! Even as a teacher myself now I can't easily characterise how 'good' it was then but I do remember a positive, friendly feel to the place and the encouragement to believe that this was a new opportunity, a fresh start. (Do secondary schools always assume that primary school life has become jaded and lacking?)

So we find ourselves in Class 1H. I still can't picture a process of getting to know new classmates. I have a much stronger recollection of our class unity. Mr Hannam, 'Derry' as we were soon to be told, was very friendly and warm. Years later I still picture him in his loose, brown cord suit (lifting at the shoulders as he pointed), pushing his glasses back up his nose, quizzically screwing up his face, telling someone how interesting their comment was and inviting others for their views too. We seem to have discussed all and everything but there were 'rules'... more of that later.

After a while I think we all knew that we had 'landed on our feet' in Mr Hannam's class. He was a bit out of the ordinary or 'cool' for today; played keyboard in a jazz band, lived on a farm, drove a Land Rover and before long we were invited to visit him and his young family at the farm on weekends. No other classes did things like that. He would often arrive in class and immediately take to the piano, with us gathered around, marvelling at his talent. A strong bond soon developed and our loyalty to him was strong. We did things that other classes didn't... I remember an assembly (I think on the Good Samaritan) when we left the stage and shook hands with pupils and staff as we progressed off to the back of the hall - which was a different to usual ending. The smiles on everyone's faces told us that we (1H) had done something a bit special.

At some point the 'class democracy system' and the 'class court' emerged. Every week we would assemble in the round, make collective decisions and address issues of behaviour. I really can't say how long it took to reach this point but I know we all bought into it. Everyone seemed to have a job. I was joint-treasurer, I suppose because my dad worked in a bank! Our small weekly 'subs' built up a fund and we agreed how to spend it. I was also responsible for the quiz and puzzle section of our class 'newspaper' (the length of the back wall and more) and took to my part with enthusiasm, inventing questions way too hard but assiduously crafted!

There was a culture of openness and questioning with clear rules as we worked on our projects for class discussion and the class 'newspaper...no such thing as a silly question, only to comment constructively etc, which must have served me very well. I was very aware of my own lack of self-confidence and under this system I thrived. I really can't recall what we learned in our infrequent formal lessons other than an obscure topic about a village in Sweden called Sodankyla and that Kiruna was a centre for iron ore! But Mr Hannam 'prophetically' told my parents that I could even go and get a degree in geography...for the 11+ failed 11/12-year-old that was bold, but maybe the planting of such seeds is all that is needed! I loved Humanities and English lessons- maths was another story!

I can't really distinguish between what happened in 1H and 2H but knowing that we would stay with Derry for a second year was a fantastic boost. By now pupils in other classes had seen what we had and must have been at least a bit envious. Over Easter 1970 Derry (his wife Debs + 3 young children) took us to the Welsh borders for a class holiday, half a class each week! We had a second trip the next year to the New Forest. The two 'half class' weeks away were memorable! In particular, I fell quite a way 'through' the branches of a fir tree as I edged farther and farther away from James C. in a game of hide and seek. Determined not to be caught I got to the point of no return and the branches gave way! I also got really worked up when I couldn't find my plates for dinner – everyone else just got on with it leaving me to search, pathetically whining about it...they were in Derry's kid's room. "Sorry old son" were his words as I joined in belatedly. But the endless 'treck' up Sugar Loaf Mountain, with the whole class finally standing atop, brought a fantastic sense of achievement. And I remember two kids sitting in the front wheel of his Land Rover, descending a 1 in 1 hill, and being swung out of a hammock in the garden by a very apologetic Sally B... none of this remarkable, but it's what I remember most.

I'm still not sure why he would put himself through that! Meeting him again, years later, I know how much he believed in his vision to rebuild lost confidence and affirm individuals who had suffered the vagaries of the secondary selection process. Pupils will inevitably respond to that degree of commitment. We knew that we were liked, respected and valued.

Derry left the school after two years but most of the class stayed together until CSEs and 'O' Levels (10) were through and I can list a lot of other teachers who were also affirming and warm and with whom many of us continued to grow. Miss M (humanities and our form tutor) was great, Andy B (drama) and a whole lot of others, so I don't want to miss the big picture. But it was those first years when much of our character was formed. One good friend's parent commented that Derry was the 'making of' some of us and I don't think that's far off!"

David's memories – "My experience in 1H and 2H was so different to my previous experience in school, I was used to teachers telling me how bad I was (spelling being an obvious area that produced a sense of despair in my teachers) and to find myself in an environment without that negativity and one in which I was also told that I was trusted by both my teacher and my fellow pupils was so positive and different.

I believe that I made more progress educationally (even my spelling!) in that two years than I had in the previous five. I was never the most confident of children and still suffer occasionally to a certain extent from a lack of confidence, but I believe that what I learnt in that safe environment that you created has helped shape my whole life. I developed much more self-belief than I had ever had before and have gone on to take various responsible positions in my private life and to be seen as someone ready to take on responsibility in my working life and have developed a successful career. I am not sure how much I would have achieved without my experience in 1H/2H."

Reading these statements (and there are others 'not for publication') invariably brings tears to my eyes. It is interesting that although both David and Andrew emphasise the importance of the relationships and Andrew places great stress on the democracy and responsibility sharing neither seems to have very strong recollections of the self-managed and self-directed approach to learning. Almost the opposite, as Andrew recalls two of the very few topics that were actually taught didactically. In fact, I did those occasional bits of conventional class teaching largely to minimise the criticism from the heads of subject departments who, correctly, suspected that I largely ignored their prescribed curriculum content. This is an issue I intend to pursue further with this group of alumni.

Chapter 6 – Creating a Democratic Class and Curriculum – Making It Up As We Went Along

Rather than impose my own idea of the kind of structures that the class democracy should have I decided that we would make it up as we went along by dealing with issues as they arose. The one thing I was clear about was the need for a class meeting. As the school required that all form teachers should appoint a boy and girl form captain from day one whose principal duties were to collect and return the class register to the school-office we had an issue to be discussed and decided straight away.

The children in my class came mainly from three different primary schools so some of them knew each other and thus had the advantage over me as to who should take up initial posts of responsibility, however minimal those responsibilities were at this stage. Not knowing that it was illegal, I decided that as well as collecting and returning the register the form captains would also have the responsibility of recording the attendances and absences in order to give them a bit more to do.

I got to the classroom early on my first day, pushed all the tables to the side of the generously sized Room 3 and arranged the chairs in a circle. I then went to the school hall to take delivery of my class. I was a bit shaken to find that the average second year class size was to be thirty-four students and that 1H had thirty-five! Twenty-six had been the most I had met on teaching practices. Fortunately, the school administration was well organised and I had already been issued with a class register with all the pupils' names, dates of birth and addresses typed into it so we were spared that rather tedious task and could get straight down to making decisions.

Having been told where to sit in their primary schools there was a bit of confusion as the students found seats in the circle and a few puzzled faces when I also sat in the circle. I told them who I was and that I was both their form teacher and their humanities teacher and that I would be working with them for about half the school week. I said that we had the whole morning together as humanities was timetabled into three half days and the whole of Friday; a major feat of imaginative time-tabling by the deputy head.

I explained that humanities consisted of history - which was everything that we knew from what was written down in the past; geography - which was about the world today; religious education - which was about what people believed; social studies – which was about how people lived together; and English - which was about how we communicated and expressed ourselves with our language.

One boy, David put his hand up and said 'That sounds like everything in the world! Are we going to study everything in the world?'

'Well that might take more time than we have,' I replied. 'I am rather hoping that you will choose to learn about the parts that really interest you and then tell the rest of us about it.'

'Will we be able to learn about anything we like then?' he asked.

'That's a really good question,' I said. 'We are going to have to talk about that!'

I then took the register and explained that in future this would be the responsibility of the form captains. The only problem being that we had not yet got any! I invited suggestions as to how we could get some. Many people spoke at once and some put their hands up so I quietly said 'we aren't going to make any decisions if we go on like this.'

I took a book from the teacher's desk and said 'all those who agree that when we are having a class discussion you only speak when you are holding the book and that until we all get to know each other we should say our name before we speak.' All agreed. This was our first vote and our first decision as a class. The problem immediately arose as to what to do when the book-holder had finished speaking. Kerry suggested that the book should be passed to someone who had their hand up chosen by the current book-holder. All agreed. This was our second decision. It worked fairly well, though there was a tendency for people to pass the book to someone they knew, which made the hand waving a bit frantic from some of the others.

David then suggested that the book should be passed to the next hand up to the left then it would be 'fair.' Again, all agreed. This was better and Andrew suggested that I as teacher should choose temporary form-captains until the class knew each other well enough to have an election. 'What is an election,' I asked. He explained, thereby creating our first example of a student teaching a lesson! I thought this was a pretty good idea but asked 'how should I choose them? I don't know who would be best any more than you do?'

Peter said that all who wanted to be a form captain could put their names on pieces of paper in a box and the first boy and girl whose names I picked out of the box would be form captains for two weeks. This time the vote was divided as Sally H wanted the trial period to be four weeks with different people doing it for a week at a time. A second vote was held to decide between Sally's suggestion and Peter's. Sally's suggestion won and so four girls names were picked out of the box. This was not necessary for the boys as only four wanted to do it.

Already we were beginning to get to know each other and learn each other's names. The level of listening and reasoning was already impressive. The democratic citizenship curriculum was creating itself!

As the number of decisions was growing I asked how were we going to remember them all? Gina said that I should write them down and put them up on the class notice-board. This was voted on and I agreed to do it, but said that I hoped I could soon hand the job over to an elected class secretary. Several people immediately offered. Mostly girls and one boy. This all took over forty minutes or so and by the time I ended the meeting over half the members of the class had spoken. Some many times. I then handed out timetables and explained which parts of the school they had to go to for various lessons that were not part of humanities.

This took us up to break time. After that I asked the class to get the chairs and tables arranged in three rows, fairly quickly, but without pushing and bashing and to choose seats quietly and without argument that could disturb neighbouring classes. Some hopes! The break bell went creating the urgency for some rapid cooperation which put an end to the chaos. Before releasing the class, I said that I thought we had a new problem to solve which was how to get the tables back and the chairs into a circle for a meeting, and vice versa, quickly and quietly in future. I asked the eight form captains if they would meet me just before the end of break to get the room ready for another class meeting after break. They agreed and all turned up early.

After break we discussed how to manage room rearrangement more efficiently. Someone suggested that it wasn't necessary and that we could have a meeting with the room in its 'normal shape' with chairs and desks in rows. Others disagreed. One of the Davids, whose mother was a teacher in the school, said that 'it was much better to be in a circle as we could all hear and see each other and it was more equal and anyway it would separate meetings from lessons.' An interesting comment as we had not had any lessons yet! Another vote was held and it was decided to meet in the circle.

I said that it was very hard to write down the decisions and at the same time manage the voting so would a form captain handle the votes in future? They offered to take it in turns. The form captain role was growing by the minute.

Then came the question of how to get the room back to its classroom configuration quickly and quietly. After discussion it was agreed that there was no magic way other than everyone having their own place at their own table in an agreed spot which they would be responsible for removing and replacing. I had not foreseen what a can of worms 'who would sit with who' could be. It was decided, with another vote, that people who had friends from primary school could sit with their friend and that I would place anyone who was left over. I wasn't too happy about this but could not think of anything better while we had three rows of five tables as the basic classroom shape. I sketched a map on the blackboard showing where everyone would be sitting once a few minutes had been spent negotiating friendship pairs.

Now we could practice classroom rearrangement in earnest. I set a target of two minutes with minimal chair scraping and collisions. That was easily achieved after several attempts, leading to a challenge from Ian that we should aim for one minute in future. We got it to 82 seconds by Wendy's smart new underwater watch, which she had won at a swimming gala in the summer holiday. That was good enough for me and lessons began with a good feeling that we had collectively solved a few problems successfully. There had been a lot of communication and learning before ever an 'official' lesson was delivered!

I issued exercise books for English and checked that everyone had something to write with. I asked the class to write about their nice memories and their not-so-nice memories of primary school. They could say anything they pleased so long as they avoided mentioning teachers by name. Next, they were to go on to write about their feelings about coming to their new school.

I explained that if anyone had any difficulties with writing they could quietly explain these to me as I walked around the class. There was no one who could not attempt the task, though some obviously launched into it with enthusiasm and others, fewer in number, were relatively hesitant. The lunchtime bell seemed to come very quickly so I said that they could carry on with their writing for homework, which school policy expected me to set three times per week. I released them row by row saying that if they had any better ideas on how to leave the classroom in an orderly fashion we could discuss them at the next class meeting. I was touched by the smiles and 'bye Mr Hannam' as they left and felt quite pleased with my first morning's work as a teacher. I knew that I had been blessed with a bright and sociable bunch of eleven-year-olds.

Humanities was not on the time-table the following day but the form captains delivered and marked the registers at form time. We all found our way to the hall for lower school assembly and all but two members of the class handed in their English books for me to read.

I realized that I had to think carefully about how to handle the school requirement that I set regular homework. I personally believed that the kids should be encouraged to carry on with their schoolwork at home if it was interesting for them to do so - and did not interfere with their other interests. I felt that it was quite a good idea for them to work independently at times but I didn't want to set homework just for the sake of it. It would not lead to the kind of relationship that I was hoping for.

I decided to discuss my dilemma at a class meeting. I would make it clear that neither I nor they could unilaterally alter or ignore school rules as I had signed a contract not to do so when I took the job. To ignore this would not be a very good model for the 'rule of law' which I wanted them to understand as part of their learning about democracy. But we could talk about different interpretations of the rules!

Reading their first pieces of writing was a shock that I suppose I should have been prepared for. The effect of failing the 11+ had been devastating for nearly all and especially, it seemed to me, for the children from what I guessed were the more aspirational middle-class families. I was nearly moved to tears by the statements from several that although their parents said they 'could do well at the secondary modern school' they nonetheless felt that they had failed their parents. They believed that they had let them down and that they might pay the price for rest of their lives.

What a dreadful burden to impose on an eleven-year-old child! I had 'passed' the 11+ with ease and had no conception of just what a sense of failure not getting a grammar school place could induce in those who were not successful. It reinforced all my previously somewhat intellectual commitment to comprehensive schools with a powerful emotional underpinning. It was a crime to subject these young undeveloped people to such an experience at this age; to demolish their self-confidence just as they were about to enter adolescence with all its attendant uncertainties and challenges.

It was all so arbitrary. If they had been born in Wales there would have been grammar school places for 30% of them whereas in our town, where people were not obviously seriously less intelligent than in Swansea (12), the figure was only 13%. In fact, it was widely known that the validity of the eleven plus tests was seriously open to challenge and probably totally unreliable. The truth of the head teacher's understanding was brought home to me and my commitment to his redeeming mission became absolute. I had a therapeutic task on my hands and not just an educational one.

Fortunately, room 3 was my teaching base for various history classes that made up the rest of my teaching load and I did not have to share it with any other teacher. This made it possible for the room to become 1H's own space. This is normal in a primary school but almost impossible in secondary schools where space is dedicated to subjects rather than groups of students. The next humanities session was on a Friday afternoon so it was possible to arrange the room in a circle for a meeting during registration and get started right away. The form captains had met the previous day, on their own initiative, and decided who would be 'on duty' on each day for the next four weeks.

It seemed very complicated to me but it worked. In fact, students of this age often seem to solve problems in ways that seem convoluted to adults. I put this down to the fact that actually they were playing at problem solving and that it was the play that mattered to them more than the solution; a process beautifully described in Peter Gray's Freedom to Learn (2013). Nonetheless, their solutions usually worked – and if they did not they would learn from their mistakes and come up with something new and better. It was much later that I discovered from the work of Jerome Bruner (1960, 1966), Lev Vygotsky and Lois Holzman (1993) that this was a classic example of Vygotsky's 'tool as result' in action. The process was what mattered. The solution was almost irrelevant; just a further opportunity to learn.

I began to feel that the more problems we faced as a class learning to live together the better. Everything was an opportunity to learn and be creative. It was an endless road of opportunity. Why had nobody told me this at the teacher's college? Could it be because they didn't know? All those lectures on 'behaviour management' were just lessons in how to deny the opportunity for self-management by individuals and the class as a collective.

I started the next class meeting by explaining that it was customary for meetings to be run by a chairman or chairwoman. Instead of a passing book it was the chair's job to ensure that only one person spoke at once and not for too long, that they kept to the point and that everyone who wanted to speak should have a chance to do so, and not just the chairperson's friends.

I said that I would chair the first meeting for a while and then hand over to the 'on duty' form captain. Nigel suggested that there should be a separate election for the chairperson as the form captains were getting all the interesting jobs. Somebody else said that we should elect a new chairperson for every meeting. Somebody else said that as it would be really good for their confidence if everybody should take it in turns to chair a meeting.

Others felt that this would be a waste of time as we would spend so much time electing chairpeople that nothing would ever get discussed. Eventually, a majority thought that as the form captains did not really have very much to do and as they wanted to be form-captains they should chair the meetings in turn until we got to know each other better. This was voted upon and agreed.

I then said that I could not chair the meeting and make notes of decisions at the same time and that we needed a class secretary as well. This led to a discussion about what qualities were required. Being able to write quickly and neatly so that everyone could read it on the class notice board were agreed to be the essential requirements. Volunteers were asked for and five girls and one boy offered. All were asked to immediately write some notes of what had been decided in the meeting so far. They were given a few minutes to do this and then the resulting pieces of paper were passed around the circle numbered one to six by me. The vote was then for the best number rather than a person by name so that people did not just vote for their friends.

To everyone's surprise, including his, Michael S received the most votes and began work immediately. He did the job so well, writing up his rough notes at home after meetings as voluntary homework, that he was re-elected time after time over the next two years. Nobody ever said 'this is a girl's job.' He had not liked his primary school much and had become upset and depressed by the death of his younger brother two years before. His mother told me that failing the eleven plus had been the last straw and that she feared for his future mental health. (50 years later he is now CEO of a successful financial services company.) She was delighted by his endless writing up of class meeting notes and encouraged him to use her type-writer. I think he was probably the first in the class to learn to type.

Throughout the two years I worked with the class he never let us down even though he was often in trouble in himself and with other teachers. I still have a large collection of his minutes of meetings and the proceedings of the class court which was to come later. From time to time he was punished by other teachers for not doing his homework but he never failed to produce the minutes of the class meeting and the class court. On one occasion when he was ill, he made his mother bring them to school to give to me personally! Probably I should have suggested that being secretary was as important as a learning opportunity as being chairperson and encouraged others to challenge Michael's monopoly. I did not do this and I am not totally sure why. Possibly because I felt that he needed the role in some deep psychological way that I did not fully understand.

Certainly, it was useful to have a committed and literate minute taker and very soon everyone in the class was writing extensively in their project work anyway, but I suspect the real reason that Michael kept the job through the whole of our two years together was that the role was so important to his identity. He was never challenged by other class members though I know that one or two would have been happy to have the job. Could it be that they recognised and respected the benefit to Michael? I don't know – but I am never surprised by the care for each other, kindness to each other, and profound moral understanding that young people can show for each other when they are free to do so. There were to be many examples of this during our time together.

The spirit that was already developing in 1H was the exact opposite of that which was imagined by William Golding in his dark novel about fascistic violence in young people, Lord of the Flies (1954), which is often held up as an example of what will inevitably happen when young people are free to develop their own self-management or self-government. I suspect that Golding's novel has more to say about the values of English public schools that normal children. For me Kohlberg in his writing about moral development in 'Just community schools' (1987) was being proved right and Golding proved wrong. More recently the Dutch writer Rutger Bregman (2019) has collected an array of evidence to contradict Golding, most notably the story of six Tongan schoolboys shipwrecked on the Pacific island of Aku in 1966.

There are those who would say that the care and kindness manifest in 1H 'was because you were there manipulating the situation and providing a safe holding environment within which the young people could safely play at democracy.' They might be right to some extent though I do not consider myself to be a particularly caring or kind person. It suggests to me that teacher training should incorporate learning experiences for more teachers to do the same! But I just do not believe that the bullying malignance of Lord of the Flies would ever have taken control of 1H and not just because of the innate kindness of most of the students. It was also because they were creating a culture of kindness. The class was learning how to stand up to occasional bullying through the democratic structures that emerged. In the adult world we need the values and strengths that grew in 1H to deal with fascism and fascist tendencies. It is hard to imagine anyone in 1H voting for Donald Trump. Certainly the one-time class members that I am in contact with would not.

Now I had a form captain as chair and a competent secretary who I could hand over minute taking to. I was now free to become a member of the meeting who put his hand up when he wanted to speak. Chairs of the meeting gradually learned that I as teacher should not automatically be chosen to speak as soon as I put my hand up. Some found this very difficult to implement however much I asked them not to give me priority. Others rather enjoyed testing out whether I really had temporarily relinquished the teacher's power to speak whenever I felt like it. In the context of the meeting or the court I explained that unless something very urgent happened, like a fire drill, I had normally handed my authority as teacher to the chair of the meeting while the meeting was in progress. If I put my hand up it meant that I was a citizen of the meeting and not 'dictator' teacher. They cautiously felt their way by daring to test that I meant what I said.

While the meeting was in session the chair was in charge and I had no more right to speak first than anybody else. I made it clear that this was not the case when I was in my role as class teacher teaching a lesson. The principle was that the democracy must not be bogus but its limits must be clear. We agreed that last lesson on Fridays would always be class meeting time and that whoever was 'in the chair' was also 'in charge' so long as they did not break the school rules – such as ending the meeting early and letting everyone go home before the rest of the school (though this was often suggested!)

In my experience children seem to be quite happy to live with the ambiguity of this situation. They accepted that this was a kind of 'play' democracy where the authority that I delegated could be reassumed by me as teacher if necessary. I never had any doubt that I could have resumed a traditional teacher/adult authority role at any time if I believed that the class was becoming 'unsafe' for any student. It was possible for the democracy to be real and yet 'held' at the same time. It could never have degenerated into a 'Lord of the Flies' situation because I would have intervened. Yet I don't think this is why it did not degenerate into this condition. I was modeling behaviour that respected the right and the space of every individual to speak and to be heard – to participate – and I think this was accepted and absorbed by the class. In a word (or three!) it was fun, it was interesting, and it was learned.

The class did not feel impelled to endlessly test me out as adolescents might if they had had no experience of this way of working when they were younger. On the other hand, if the teacher does not join the 'play' and behave 'as if' they had surrendered their authority then I don't think the democracy would work and lead to important learning. I was like a drama teacher who was able to step in and out of role – in role as participant citizen then 'out of role' as teacher in charge.

My long-term aim was to create as many posts of responsibility as possible and to regularly subject them to re-election so that it would be almost impossible for anyone not to have some experience of at least one job over the year. In reality this was more than possible because the class continually created additional jobs which they would volunteer to do, and which often did not call for a class election. Some examples were organiser of the class fashion shows, or chess tournaments, or lunchtime discos, or five-a-side football challenges, or editor of endless columns in the class newspaper. Overall editor of the class newspaper was always an elected post though, as were other key roles such as keyholder of the class games cupboard or class timekeepers - and many of these elected officers also had elected deputies. Over the two years of 1H/2H there was nobody who did not have at least one 'job', many had two or three and a few played many roles.

Once we got the curriculum rolling, the class and I negotiated the seating arrangements around the needs of different kinds of activities of which there were basically two. When they were working to curriculum decided by me, they would sit in groups basically of their choice but I would accept no argument if I wanted to place a new student, or one who had few friends, in a particular group. I explained to the meeting that much could be learned by sharing ideas with each other and I did not want anyone to sit alone and be left out. I answered questions about it but in the end made it clear that I was going to make this decision as teacher responsible for the well-being and learning of everyone in the class. This was never seriously challenged and hurtful or rejecting behaviour towards less popular students was very rare.

I carried out regular sociograms where everyone was asked to secretly name the two people in the class that they would most like to work with. This gave me a powerful understanding of who was popular and who was isolated. Overtime the 'popular' tended to stay popular but the 'isolates' definitely became less isolated.

When the class was working on curriculum generated by them around topics and questions of interest to them then the groups would be created from those sharing the interest, and I would accept people working on their own if they were the only one with that interest. Often these were the most isolated students at first, but gradually they became less isolated as the class began to cohere as a group. They became accepted as 'characters' with some odd tendencies. Probably at any time three quarters of the class would be working in groups and eight or nine would be working alone.

Although we had a fairly large classroom with a fair bit of storage there was not enough space or tables for every individual to have a two-seat table to themselves. A group working on 'navies in Roman times' might have two tables with four people around it whereas individuals working on 'secret codes' and another researching the 'history of clothes' might have to share a table.

Right from the start of our time together I had said that as we were spending quite a bit of class time learning about things and questions that we found very interesting it would be a good idea to share them with the rest of the class. Everyone, including the shyest, agreed with this when I put it to one of our earliest class meetings. Although individuals and groups were not always ready when they promised to be nobody ever refused to 'teach their topic' except for the few occasions when somebody had chosen an issue about which almost no source material was available. Sometimes a parent or other adult would be invited to assist with a presentation.

Arguments did occur, as would be expected, and there were differences of opinion about the noise level in the room at times. Some said I was too strict and some said it was too noisy. The same people sometimes said both at different times. This was a perfect subject for the Friday meeting agenda! I told the meeting that I set the noise level at what I was comfortable with at the time and if I was tired, I would sometimes insist on silence. 'Can you think of a better way to set the noise level?' I asked.

Christine suggested that it would be more democratic if people could put their hands up if they found it too noisy and then it would depend on how the pupils felt and not just me. I asked how I would know whether the 'hand-up' meant a need for quiet or need for my help as teacher. David K said that the left hand could mean quiet and the right hand could be a request for my help. I pointed out that if the room had to be quiet for just one pupil then that was no more democratic than if I wanted it quiet to suit me. Tim suggested that if five left hands went up it should be followed by five minutes of no talking.

'How would we know when the five minutes is up?'

'Mr Hannam can tell us.'

I said that 'I am not too happy to do this as I want to be helping people not watching the clock.'

It was decided that Wendy with the big watch was elected unopposed to the post of class time-keeper. It would be the form captains' job to count the left hands going up and when it reached five they would call for 'five minutes quiet.' When it was up the timekeeper would call 'five minutes up.'

Next Monday morning was a humanities session and in my opening remarks I said nothing about the new noise level rule but just waited to see if the system would work. Nobody had forgotten the decision of the previous Friday meeting which Michael, the class secretary, had pinned up on the class notice board at registration time in his best writing and in great detail as '1H LAW NUMBER ONE.'

Well, as might be expected on a Monday morning, everybody had lots to say to each other and the room soon became quite noisy. I did nothing as the decibels passed the point of my idea of a good working environment. Suddenly seven or eight hands shot up – mainly left hands too. The duty form captain Andrew duly pronounced 'five minutes quiet' and a near- total hush came over the room. Gradually, people began to whisper, until Wendy announced 'five minutes up.' This went on in all the humanities sessions of the week with quiet times being called about twice per lesson. I was absolutely amazed by the success of the scheme as I had not once had to tell the class to be quiet.

Imagine my shock when on Friday morning Michael pinned up the agenda for the afternoon class meeting. Item one was 'The hands-up system is not working. Something needs to be done. RJ, CE, AD SG' – these being the initials of the four students who had asked Michael to put the item on the agenda.

At the meeting it quickly emerged that these four and many others were annoyed that people were whispering in quiet times. They were not as impressed as I was by the absence of open talking and the generally undistracting environment that had been created without me having to say a word. The fact that I was pleased that the law was achieving its purpose and that the whispering in quiet times was not disturbing anyone was not the point so far as the objectors, and many others it transpired, were concerned.

'It's not fair,' they argued. 'It is the same people who whisper all the time and if everybody did it none of us would be able to get on with what we are doing. What's the point in having a class law if it does not apply to everybody?'

Of course, they were quite right and had taken to heart my earlier comments about the 'rule of law' applying to everybody. They easily won the vote for enforcement at the meeting – even some of the most frequent 'whisperers' voted for it! I think the idea of being able to hand out 'punishments' seemed to make some of the class feel that now they really did have some power.

The four concerned had a plan and it was no coincidence that they were all form captains. Their proposal was that the two duty form captains should each record the names of whisperers in the back of their rough work notebooks and that I as teacher should set the offenders 'lines' to write as a punishment with a tariff of ten lines for every time somebody whispered during a week.

I must say I was not too keen to be put into this role especially as I really thought that writing lines was a complete waste of time. I was corrected by David K.

'That's the whole point of setting 'lines' to be written. It is supposed to waste their time otherwise it would not be a punishment.'

I argued that the 'punishments' should do something useful for the community but David won the day for the hardliners with the riposte, 'If lines stop the whispering in quiet times that will be good for the community.'

Several people objected that the form captains would not put their friends 'in the book.' I then explained that in real life the law was enforced by the police, in this case the form captains, but that justice and punishments were handed out by the courts of law. It was the job of a court to consider the evidence carefully and give the 'accused' the chance to defend themselves against the charge.

'Let's have a court then,' proposed James C.

This was discussed at some length and the meeting ended at the end of the school day without a decision being agreed. We decided to continue the discussion at the next Friday meeting and in the mean-time everyone would find out as much as they could about how courts worked for that week's homework. In fact, preparing for a meeting discussion often became homework and nobody seemed to object. I learned from several parents that some members of the class spent a great deal of time on research which included interrogating them and often asking questions that they the parents did not know the answers to, such as 'who chooses the magistrates and judges in the English court system?'

During the next week seven people had their names in the form captains' rough books for whispering or talking in quiet times, mostly once or twice, but in Lawrence's case eleven times! On the following Friday I allowed enough time for a meeting and a sitting of the class court should one be created. The form captains explained the totals of their 'bookings' and it was decided to set up a court that would sit after Friday class meetings if there were any cases to hear.

It was obvious that many pupils had found out something about 'courts' and several had read and cut out local magistrate court reports from the local newspaper. Andrew created a special exhibition space on the class notice board called 'What courts are for' and put all the cuttings up. Three pupils were elected as class magistrates from about ten volunteers. I was very impressed that after working with these children for a month these three would almost certainly be the ones that I would have chosen. Two of them had been form captains during the trial period and it was decided that nobody could hold two such important offices at the same time so two new form captains who were not magistrates were elected for the rest of the term. This fitted neatly with my lesson on real life law where policemen could not also be magistrates or judges.

I went on to explain how a jury worked. If the accused pleaded guilty then the magistrates just had to decide on a suitable response but if they pleaded not guilty the meeting decided that the rest of the class would vote as a jury. The results would be recorded by the class secretary, whose job was rapidly expanding. It was further decided that an offender would only have to appear before the class court if they had been put 'in the book' at least five times in a week.

The court duly sat, with a special table for the magistrates who had a carpenters hammer as gavel that had been left in the room by the caretaker. Another table became 'dock' before which the accused would stand while the jury, which included me and the rest of the class, sat in a semi-circle behind the accused but facing the magistrates. Nearly everybody had watched courtroom dramas on TV.

The first and only defendant, Lawrence, said he was 'not guilty' as he had only been borrowing rubbers and pencils and anyway at the time he didn't know that there would be a court and possible consequences. He had a good constitutional point against retrospective legislation of course and I supported him in the proceedings. However, the magistrates disagreed and I decided not to intervene as I had already prepared time for the court to sit and allowed expectations to rise. (With hindsight I think I was probably wrong in doing this.)

Lawrence was found guilty by a majority vote of the jury. The magistrates conferred and said that as this was his first offence and as they had not yet had time to discuss with Mr Hannam what punishments they were allowed to give he would just be told not to talk in quiet times in future. There was some sense of anti-climax in the jury, some of whom might have been hoping for a hanging, but Lawrence seemed relieved and promised to obey the court's instruction in future. Something he, and one or two other 'serial whisperers', had great difficulty in doing for the next two years!

Many meetings were later spent discussing the purpose and suitability of punishments and what was meant by 'justice'. Were they meant to deter and how did deterrence square with justice? Should there always be a 'community service' aspect to punishments? Should restitution be a part of it? Should mitigating circumstances be taken into account? If somebody had been provoked, were they entirely responsible for their own actions? I still have contemporary notes of these discussions and find it hard to believe that these kids were only 11/12 years old and that they were supposed to be 'non-academic.' It was a major self-directed programme of citizenship education and gave me endless opportunities to explain the legal concepts involved in answer to their questions.

More laws were passed. Eventually there were fourteen of them. Some were very specific. For example, 'only form captains or Mr Hannam can mark the register.' Others were very general. 'Nobody is allowed to hit, swear at or bully another person.' Offences against specific laws would be brought to the class court by the class official concerned but breaches of general laws could be reported by any member of the class to a form captain, who would prosecute the case on their behalf.

This later developed into a system whereby anyone could make their complaint in writing on the court notices section of the class notice board. I always made it clear that the class meeting could not pass a law that conflicted with the law of England or the official school rules. This 'do it yourself' practical justice system proved to be remarkably close to the Judicial Committee (JC) process used in Sudbury Valley model democratic schools that I have since visited in many countries (Greenberg 1992).

While the social learning involved in the creation of the democratic classroom was emerging very quickly the lesson content side of the curriculum was more constrained.

The head teacher wished to see some sort of integrated curriculum. He might even have been persuaded that it could be to some extent co-constructed with the pupils. The heads of subject department certainly did not. They feared loss of status along with loss of control of part of their curriculum territory.

The new head of lower school who chaired the first-year humanities team meetings had his own ideas about how history and geography could be linked while still taught as discrete subjects. The heads of those subject departments were more or less happy with this. He had never taught English however and here he bowed to the prescriptions coming from the head of that department. None of this allowed much scope for the students to pursue their own interests in depth as self-directed learning, asking more and more profound questions, which was what I wanted to see happen. Nonetheless, no attempt was made to impose a subject timetable on each class so there was still a fair bit of flexibility and I made maximum use of it.

I could not entirely ignore the team generated history and geography curriculum as a number of whole year trips were planned around it which otherwise would have made no sense to my class, so I squeezed it into the minimum possible time. I created my own bank of resources for this team curriculum to enable the class to work in groups exploring the material through their own questions. I set their investigations into context with a small amount of factual teaching from the front. The groups would sometimes choose to study one issue which they would present to the rest of the class and at other times individuals in the group would pursue their own questions or write their own stories. These would then be included in a collective piece of work.

The prescribed and very tedious English exercises and tasks I substantially ignored. I thought that the class was doing plenty of writing already and was developing very good communication skills and extending their vocabulary through the participative democracy. I had a private reading time at the end of every half day when pupils were encouraged to read stories rather than non-fiction and to write reviews for the class newspaper.

The newspaper quickly covered the whole back wall of the classroom and spread along the side wall that had no windows. By half term there were sports (several), fashion, book review, quizzes and puzzles, jokes and cartoons, poetry, transport, pets and bird watching, ponies and many other columns each with its own editor.

Sometimes I would teach a short poetry lesson based on my enthusiasms or a poem recommended by a pupil. These lessons, to my surprise, were very popular and led to lots of poems being written for voluntary homework. Several class poetry anthologies were created and printed into booklets. The head of art read these and often used them as stimuli for art lessons.

Sometimes I would read a book to the class and sometimes students would read parts of a book that they found exciting or just talk about a book that they were reading. Sometimes I would be asked to read all or part of a book chosen by a class member. Parts of the catchment area were quite middle-class and I had several avid readers and reviewers in the class. The idea that reading and then reviewing what you had read was fun spread around the whole class.

Compulsion, coercion and punishment for failure would have been totally unnecessary and counter-productive. I kept extensive but somewhat secret notes on what everyone was doing but despite sometimes being asked resolutely refused to give marks or grades beyond 'wow – I enjoyed that'. My notes were most useful to keep the head teacher and parents happy though this became less and less necessary for parents as they saw what their children were doing at home.

Once the official humanities team curriculum, the meeting and court, and the reading times and poetry sessions were in place between a third and a half of humanities time was available for the pursuit of individual interest projects, which were presented to the class as they were completed. This probably represented an average of around 20-25% of total school curriculum time. These project presentations provided a steady flow of student taught lessons which often happened on Friday afternoons before the class meeting and, if there were any cases, the class court.

The head teacher once chose to visit my classroom just as a group that had studied 'firefighting' set light to a model of a seventeenth century London house built of wood and straw to demonstrate the spread of the Great Fire of London in 1666. It was safely placed on a metal tray standing on two bricks and they quickly extinguished the flames with model hand pump engines made from water pistols. I had a bucket of water handy just in case. I think I was lucky with this head teacher. Far from reading the riot act to the class he asked some interesting questions and congratulated the students on their 'vividly interesting' lesson. He also told me afterwards never to do anything like that again inside the building as it was lucky the fire alarm had not gone off and finished off learning for the whole school for the rest of the day!

Maybe at this point I should include a summary of the personal, social and civic learning that I believed to be taking place after just six weeks of the first half-term which more than justified the time spent on meetings and courts.

The most obvious was probably the confidence that developed in all the students in their ability to articulate their thoughts and feelings and express them to others. The belief that they had something important to contribute and that it would be heard by others – the teacher and their peers. This developed along with a sense of responsibility which arose from realising that what they said could influence events in a way that they would actually have to take responsibility for. They became responsible through being given and accepting responsibility.

As a teacher I am perfectly capable of 'controlling' a class in the conventional manner which involves 'repressing' potential misbehaviour through strength of personality, experience and, as a last resort, punishments. The students are afraid to disobey and so long as they are not too afraid a purposeful lesson can take place in an orderly environment. It was my belief that this approach denied the class the opportunity to learn how to manage itself as a community and thus to learn important lessons of citizenship. These include the need to work together democratically to decide and legislate for what kind of community they want to live in, to elect an executive to implement those decisions and, if necessary, to act together to defend law and order through a democratic jury based judicial system.

All this existed in my classroom. I chose to allow a bit of chaos to emerge, not difficult when thirty-five eleven-year-olds are contained in one room against their will in a compulsory school system, in order to use it as a resource for learning. Normally in schools where teacher authority rules in the classroom chaotic behaviour only surfaces in the relatively uncontrolled context of the playground or the school bus where bullying and reigns of fear can occur as the strong vent their feelings on the weak and anti-social acts go unchallenged.

Quite quickly, and certainly before the first half-term holiday, what little disturbing or anti-social behaviour that there was was not being contained by me but by the peer group. I believe that the democratic atmosphere of the class meant that there was very little serious anti-social behavior to deal with but inevitably, with 35 young people and one adult in one room for hours on end, it was guaranteed that there would be some. The students, or enough of them to make it work, had learned that when they worked together through appropriate structures and processes which they had participated in creating they could deal with problems themselves.

Although I was usually there as back-up, they gradually learned that they could solve problems, without me. At first my presence gave them the security to know and feel that, if it was too much for them, I would intervene to support them. As time went by I found that my actual presence was less and less necessary. Although this approach takes up a fair amount of time it offers priceless opportunities for important learning in itself and also frees the teacher to work closely with individual students who need help. In creating an orderly environment through the democratic cultivation of self-restraint purposeful learning can flourish without fear or adult coercion.

This was not just my view but also that of a growing group of very supportive parents. Far from complaining about my apparently unusual methods I was already receiving very positive feedback from a number of parents who saw the self-esteem and self-confidence returning to their children after the '11+' disaster. They were delighted to hear about the self-restraint and self-government that was developing in the democratic classroom. Several comments were passed to the head teacher, including some requests from parents of students in other classes for transfers into my already overcrowded class. This probably explained the support that he always provided and the interest that he always showed - though it did not always make for easy relations with all my colleagues.

The head teacher was not happy about teachers leaving their classrooms during lesson time. As my class became more and more self-managing towards the end of the first term I got into the habit of visiting the school library to find a book or to check something, or to use the school phone, feeling confident that all would be well on my return to the classroom. I regarded this as a useful test for the self-management system that was emerging. As it was against the school rules for younger students to visit the library alone or in groups during lessons, a rule that I felt to be singularly stupid, I would sometimes accompany a student or a group who wanted to research a topic.

On one occasion I was summoned to the head as a result of this. He told me that he had called into my classroom to see how I was getting on as it was coming up to the end of my first term. He had found the class working in silence yet I was not in the room. The form captains had told him that 'Mr Hannam has gone to the library and because it was getting a bit noisy, we are having a quiet time.' He accepted this without further question and left the room. He had waited outside for a few moments to see if disorder broke out as he half expected. It didn't and he returned to his office.

He said 'I have two questions for you Derry. Firstly, what on earth is a 'quiet time', and secondly do you know that staff are not supposed to leave their classes unsupervised?'

'But they were supervised,' I replied. 'They were supervising themselves. A quiet time is something they have created to keep the noise down when they are working on their projects.'

It says a lot for the man that he just accepted this with a resigned, 'I hope I am going to be able to live with your appointment Derry. That's all for now.'

A few months later the capacity of the class to make itself quiet led to another summons to the head. This one was more difficult and highlights the problem of creating a democratic self-governing class in a school where such an approach is not the norm.

1H had a mathematics teacher who had great difficulty in controlling all her classes. She rapidly resorted to shouting at kids to be quiet and this just made them noisier. She shouted at 1H and they rather resented it – especially as several students actually wanted to learn some mathematics.

Although I had told the class that their laws only applied in my lessons, I obviously had not made the point strongly enough because they called for a quiet time in a maths lesson. Apparently, a number of hands went up as the room became noisy. The teacher demanded to know what was going on. The form captains later explained to me that the timekeeper announced 'five minutes quiet' and the room became silent. She then shouted at them to tell her what was going on. No-one would answer. It was a quiet time. Eventually one of the form captains explained that 'this is what we do in Mr Hannam's lessons when it is too noisy.' Instead of saying 'that's a good idea, you can do the same in my lessons' she announced that what they did in Mr Hannam's lessons was up to Mr Hannam but in her class they were to be quiet when she said so.

That might just have been the end of the matter but unfortunately a very honest but forthright girl called Rosalyn observed 'But Miss when you shout at us nobody takes any notice.' It was no more than the truth but great offence was taken by the teacher who complained to her union representative that I was undermining discipline in her class.

There were two unions in the school in what seemed to me to be a permanent power struggle for members. The maths teacher was in one and I was in the other. Without telling me her union representative complained to the head teacher about my 'unprofessional' behaviour in telling my class how to behave in other teachers' lessons.

He explained why I had been summoned to his office. He was his usual reasonable and slightly ironic self. When I told him that I had told the class that our democratic laws were only for my lessons I have no doubt that he believed me. He said he would tell the union representative that it was up to me how I 'controlled' my classes but that he had made it clear to me that as their form teacher I must make it clear to my class that each teacher had their own methods which must be respected. He took some responsibility on himself as he had created the 'integrated humanities teacher' role. Perhaps he had not realised that the children would think of the methods of the teacher who taught them for over half the school week as the 'normal' methods. 'We live and learn,' he said,' and Derry you might like to learn that if you are going to do things in a democratic way, and I am behind you when you do, it would be a good idea to explain what you are doing to the other teachers who teach the class.'

At the time I was very grateful to him for his support as when I first heard of the union complaint I thought I might be fired! Later, however, I wondered if he should not have taken a bit more of a grip on the situation himself. If he wanted me to do things in a democratic and self-directing way then with his years of experience, he could or should have foreseen the dangers and advised me more carefully before incidents occurred.

I was to meet this problem again in my next two posts and then see it from the other side when I became a deputy head myself. This is probably easier said than done though as my 'methods' were not carefully pre-planned and out of a text-book. I was making it up as I went along – or rather the kids were!

Visits to my classroom from the head became fairly regular. One visit was especially hilarious with hindsight. This time he arrived in my classroom with a group of five teachers from another school which was considering setting up a similar humanities programme to ours. Once again, I was not in the room and the class were working in an orderly way on their projects and supervising themselves. They were having a 'quiet time' and I was in the school library helping someone to find a book. A visitor observed "There is no teacher here yet the class seems to be working quietly on its own. What's going on. Where is the teacher?"

The same Andrew who contacted me on Facebook fifty years later was at the time an elected form-captain and chair of the class meeting .He replied to the visitor "Well you see our class teacher Mr Hannam is a bit soft and if we didn't have our own class government it would be chaos in here!" I reminded him of this helpful comment at a dinner party for class alumni, held at his house many years later. He was embarrassed and said "Help. I actually remember saying that. I could poke my eye out!!" The rest of us just had a very good laugh about it, as did the Head and I years before when he told me what Andrew had said after the visitors had left. I think I was very lucky to work for that man.

He knew very well that I was going through the motions and not seriously following the prescribed curriculum of the component subject departments of the 1H humanities schedule. He was genuinely interested in the motivation of the students who were, by the end of the first term, substantially following their own interests individually or in groups for at least half of their humanities time. Additionally, they were working in investigatory collaborative groups for history and geography topics.

Everything was built around questions asked by the students and thus their purposes were both their own and each others'. A great deal of fiction and non-fiction writing was for the class newspaper which extended to every inch of wall that was not window or blackboard. Poetry and short story writing became almost a craze. Almost everybody was both writing and responsible for editing some column or other and should anyone dare to pin something up without consent of the appropriate editor then it would inevitably lead to a case for the court.

There were endless presentations, discussions, reading book reviews and extracts as well as the proceedings of the class meetings and the class court. Poetry became very popular, both reading, writing and reciting. Many students loved haikus, perhaps in some cases because they did not have to write much. Though I remember that one of the Davids who had written very little in primary school became fascinated by the three-line form of the haiku and spent hours at home explaining to his parents how, if you worked to perfect it, you could say so much in few words.

A number of anthologies were produced through the two years we were together and these were often used as stimulation by the head of the art department. Homework was rarely set formally by me but the students knew it was school policy and most accepted my request that they continued with something that was interesting to them for two sessions of 20-30 minutes per week. Some did much, much, more though I rarely checked.

There is now plenty of research to show that homework is essentially useless as practised in most school systems and that children can make better use of their own time. Teachers are likewise relieved of the burden of endless 'marking' of useless busywork. I did very little or no conventional 'marking' in the sense of writing on students' work. I felt that it was slightly offensive and preferred to send them notes or just talk about it.

The head was fulsome in praising what he saw. 'It's what I want for all the first-year classes.' He told me that he intended to make me 'head of first year humanities' and to increase my salary from the third term of my first year. Unfortunately, he forgot to discuss this idea with my immediate boss who was head of lower school humanities out of whose 'territory' my patch would be carved. When he was told he protested that he wanted to take the first year again and that I could take the present first year into the second year. I was very happy with that as it meant that I could continue my work with 1H for another year and spread the ideas into the whole year group.

Some of the other teachers in the first-year team had been watching what I had been doing and were keen to take part and keep their classes for another year too – though that was not universal. The ones who thought I was crazy or that my approach might be hard to replicate were able to either become part of a new team around my boss and induct the new first year, or else leave the lower school humanities project altogether, which two of the seven did.

The head teacher was fighting off more criticism from the established heads of department for the humanities subjects than I had realised. It led to some fairly hostile comments in the staff room. To face them down and to justify continuing the approach into the second year the head decided to run a combined general knowledge/verbal reasoning test with all the first-year students. It was called the Bristol Achievement Test. I had never heard of it; nor have I heard of it since. But it was a pet test of the head teacher. I suspect he also wanted to reassure himself that my class would do no worse than the other classes. He was delighted with the results which showed the whole year doing better than would be expected for students of their age.

I was rather embarrassed by the fact that my class emerged with substantially higher scores than any of the others. It could well have been just luck or possibly caused by the fact that the students had been placed into classes on a geographical basis rather any academic form of grouping and, maybe, I had a higher proportion of middle-class professional families in my class. I suppose the test result was what I had hoped for but nonetheless it was hard for a teacher in their probationary year to live with and led to more staffroom comments such as '...of course D (the head) gave him the class with all the middle class kids in it.'

I knew that I was taking a chance in setting up the 1H democratic learning community. It might fail catastrophically and get me fired. It had never occurred to me that living with success could be just as difficult. When the union that I was not a member of heard that the head intended to give me a pay rise in my third term they submitted a formal complaint pointing to a regulation in the teachers' pay and conditions that said that teachers could not be promoted during their probationary year.

'Bloody marvelous!' I thought. 'A union objecting to a pay-rise for a young teacher!!' As a result, I didn't get the cash until my second year.

Chapter 7 – The Democratic Class becomes a Democratic Year Group of seven Classes

As the first year came to an end the following year's second-year humanities team was formed. I was put in charge of it and also became pastoral year head making me responsible for the overall well-being of all 230 second year students. The second-year humanities team consisted of four members of the first-year team who wanted to take their classes for a second year, together with a history teacher already in the school who was excited by what he saw happening, plus two new appointments straight from university. These teachers also became the form guidance tutors for their humanities classes.

My immediate boss, as head of lower school humanities, also came to some of our second- year team planning meetings. I had initially been a bit anxious about this but in fact he proved to be a big-hearted and generous person who quickly recovered from his understandable annoyance at the way I had been promoted without his involvement in the decision. He was a very effective teacher with some ten years of experience who was also a bit of a maverick in his own way. He was known to do handstands or other gymnastic tricks in front of a class if he felt a lesson was getting a bit boring, and to continue to talk upside down. Interest recovered sharply!

Kids loved him and I admired him when he talked quite openly to me about trying to introduce some of my ideas into his class. 'I find it hard to really shut up and listen to the kids. I think I'm a bit of a showman and I enjoy being centre-stage too much. I think I have developed some bad habits. Experience isn't everything is it – especially if it has been the wrong experience.'

I felt – 'I like you mate and I would be happy for you to teach my kids.' Later as a school manager and an inspector I found this capacity to reflect on practice to be quite rare in the teaching profession. It has become rarer in English state schools under pressure from our current prescribed curriculum, high stakes testing and performance target environment.

I explained to the team how my democratic approach worked and expressed the hope that we could achieve some commonalty of purpose through the whole year group of seven classes. I stressed there was no expectation that everyone would implement the whole package. I made it clear that my class had 'made it up as we went along' and that they should feel free to do the same. All agreed to have class meetings and some wanted to also experiment with the court idea. We agreed to create a second-year students' council with representatives from all seven classes which would meet weekly at lunchtimes. We would all try to attend at least once every three weeks so that there were always two teachers present. We were fortunate in being given a one-hour weekly team planning period as part of our individual schedules.

I was unhappy about the fact that the classes of two of the teachers who had dropped out of the team were also the classes that had had the most incidents of anti-social behaviour and bullying. Because the more experienced team members wanted to continue with their first- year classes I felt that really I should leave 1H and take one of the 'difficult' classes myself giving the other 'difficult' class to the experienced history teacher who was joining the team. This would avoid the two beginners having to take on 'difficult' classes. He agreed to do this but I chickened out under some parental and student pressure to stay with 1H - now 2H. As penance I took the three most 'difficult' kids into my class pushing it up to an absurd 37, leaving the strongest looking of the beginners with a group of 29. Fortunately, two families from 1H and one of the 'difficult' families moved house over the summer so in the end it was only 34 again and I did not have to cope with the hostile opinions of the maths and science teachers when they were forced to teach an overlarge 2H.

The 2H students told me that their new maths teacher had told them that they '...need not think that you can try any of your democratic nonsense while I am in charge.' He also discussed with them whether they thought that it was a 'good idea' to have me as their humanities teacher for two years; clearly suggesting that he thought it was wrong. He was giving them the opportunity to criticise my methods. I don't think he had much success. As far as the 2H students were concerned the democratic methods were theirs not mine. He was the head of the mathematics department and had been very openly hostile to me in the staff room over the incident with the 1H maths teacher the previous year.

Amazingly the unions accepted the existence of classes of over 30 in the younger years as a trade-off for much smaller classes in the older and more troublesome age groups. I must admit that I had not given enough thought to the effect on other teachers of my manipulation of the class lists. Neither had I been sufficiently aware that the rest of the staff were beginning to divide into two camps in their attitude to what was becoming known as the 'second year humanities democratic experiment' or 'Derry's crazies' depending on the point of view.

A parallel polarisation was happening in staff attitudes to me personally. With hindsight I feel that the head teacher should probably have insisted that I explain what we were up to to the rest of the staff, but he went on secondment to a bigger job as the project moved into its second year, and he was not in the school for much of the third semester of our first year. He was replaced by an ambitious and determined deputy as acting head who was personally very supportive, partly I suspect because he wanted to use my experiment to support his own bid for headship elsewhere. A combination of inexperience, and perhaps overlarge ego, supported by the enthusiasm of the students, their parents, and colleagues in the second-year team impelled me forward in a semi-intoxicated state of mind!

I honestly do not know whether it would have been better to be much more upfront and explicit with the whole staff right from the start about what I wanted to do. I do know that it would have been extremely difficult for a teacher in their first or even second year of teaching to do this. It may be that just slowly 'doing it' and then managing any flak that flew as creatively and constructively as possible was realistically the best that could be done. It would take a brave head teacher to publicly announce what I intended when he was barely sure of where it would go himself, especially as I and the class 'were making it up as we went along.' He, and his successor in our second year, and my line manager chose to give me a safe but unpublicised space to work in. I think that that in itself was a very brave thing to do.

I had persuaded the head teacher to schedule the whole humanities second year at the same time. We were allocated a suite of seven more or less adjacent rooms as our team base that provided a communal territory. We also had the use of the school hall and a drama room. The team planned to 'contain' the politically unavoidable geography content to as small a time as possible as discrete lessons. This was in deference to the demands of the head of the geography department who was also the head of lower school, my line manager, and himself leading the new first year humanities team. It is ironic that forty years later all Andrew remembers of lesson content is an extraordinarily boring (I thought) worksheet on Finnish industry in Rovaniemi!

Meanwhile the head of English was quite bitter about his subject being handed over to people he called 'lunatics' for two years and not just one so he gave up even attempting to prescribe English content to the humanities teams. That was a great relief!

The head of history, who was another of my bosses for my work with older history classes, took a different tack. He was an Australian with an ironic sense of humour, no ambition for headship, and plans to retire and travel home overland. He became both interested in and supportive of what was developing in the lower school humanities classes. He told me not to worry too much about his curriculum requirements as he was impressed that many of the kids chose projects that had historical angles anyway and he liked their enquiring attitudes and confident presentations.

The head of religious studies took a similar view and expressed support for the moral learning that was taking place through the class democracies. This meant that not only were the second year humanities teachers freed from a great deal of prescribed subject curriculum content from above but that we as a team could generate our own collective and individual material and, most importantly, individuals and groups of students from different classes could choose to work for extended periods of time on their own self-directed projects.

As all the classes were based in more or less adjacent rooms students could drift in and out of the rooms to seek help from any one of the seven teachers. As we also had the use of the school hall teachers could give lectures to as many students as wanted to attend on subjects close to their hearts or topics requested by the students. Sometimes other teachers, parents, and 'experts' from the community would give these lectures which were always entirely optional for the students. I guess I was modeling this on my year at Oxford University where any student could attend any lecture on any subject that interested them.

These second-year humanities lectures became very popular and sometimes they were given by teachers from outside the humanities team. On one occasion a science teacher gave a talk on the history of local railways that was attended by over a hundred students. Humanities teachers would sometimes attend these lectures because there were always enough other team members to work with the kids who stayed in their classrooms. The classroom doors were rarely shut. An important spin-off was that this arrangement was of enormous benefit to the two new young teachers who just fell into the larger calm and purposeful atmosphere of the team.

Chapter 8 – 2H hits the national press – The visit to the SUN

It was a few months into the second year that my first brush with 'the press' occurred. I did not handle it very wisely but it ended well. The mother of one of the 1H (now 2H) boys came to see me to say that she had a cousin who was a reporter on the Sun national newspaper. She had been telling him about the class democracy and he thought there was a story in it. He wanted to know if he could come to a class meeting with a photographer. I naively said yes, so long as the class agreed. I was vaguely aware that I should probably tell the head teacher but he was no longer in the school. He was seconded to the local authority for a year to develop lower school humanities courses in other schools and I was unsure how to contact him.

The school was being run day-to-day by the senior deputy head who I did not know so well. He had a rather fierce and authoritarian reputation with both staff and students though I got on well with him personally. He was not unsupportive of what I was doing as he was impressed with the good sense and order of my class and the whole year group. He had attended a meeting of the second-year students' council at his request and both he and they were impressed by the interest each showed in the work of the other.

I put off telling him about the press visit until the day before and of course, as luck would have it, he was visiting another school that day. In the end I informed the senior mistress that somebody from a newspaper was coming to talk to my class was that OK. I don't think she realised they were coming to get a story and I was certainly not very clear in my explanation. I was hiding behind ambiguity. She just assumed that they were coming as visitors to talk with the second-year humanities classes. Visitors were doing this all the time and as there was no formal system for getting consent for such visits, she didn't give it another thought.

The class were very excited by the prospect of 'getting in the newspaper' and certainly none had objected to the visit. The form captains planned a short speech of welcome before beginning the Friday afternoon meeting, which had a fairly full agenda. There were only two cases for the court to follow the meeting. One very minor one involved Stephen D putting up a report for the class newspaper on the latest second year inter-class football match without obtaining the prior consent of the sports editor, David C.

The other was more unusual and puzzling. Chris C, an amateur dramatics enthusiast who ran the class drama club, did not normally get 'put in the book' for talking in quiet times yet in the week prior to the press visit he managed to break just about every class law and do an awful lot of inappropriate talking and interrupting. And then it dawned on me. He had contrived to be 'in the dock' for the court sitting which he hoped would pretty well guarantee not just getting his name but also his photograph in the Sun. It worked.

The reporter, Peter Game, arrived on time and was met by the students and brought to Room 3 just in time for the Friday class meeting. Reporter and photographer played along with the class 'system' very well. They listened attentively to the speech of welcome and then gave a short talk about their work for a national newspaper. Peter asked if he could sit in the meeting circle and if the photographer could move around looking for good angles. The chair agreed 'so long as you put your hand up to speak – like everyone else – including Mr Hannam.' The meeting began. Peter took a few notes and one or two pictures were taken. The visitors did not seem to be terribly interested in the proceedings to this point.

Then the sitting of the court began with the magistrates taking their places. At this the pressmen came to life and I realised what they had really come for. The first case involved Stephen's failure to seek the appropriate editor's consent before putting an article up on the class newspaper wall. Peter made some interesting observations to the magistrates when they asked him if arguments between journalists and editors happened in 'real life' newspapers. He explained that arguments were non-stop at the Sun and that reporters could seriously fall out with each other if somebody's pet story got pushed off the front page by somebody else's. The case was dismissed because Stephen, the accused, persuaded the magistrates that the sports editor had given him permission to pin up second year match reports at the beginning of the year when they had been friends, but that now they had fallen out he had changed his mind.

Then came the Chris case and a long list of charges were read out by the form captains and the class 'quiet book keeper.' The Sun reporter was scribbling furiously now and the photographer was taking shot after shot. 'How do you plead?' asked David H the chief magistrate. 'Not Guilty' replied Chris barely keeping the smile off his face as the photographer knelt on the floor in front of him for a close-up. By this time the magistrates had worked out what he was up to and asked him to explain why there were so many charges against him. 'I was just doing it for fun and anyway knocking the chairs over was an accident.'

At this point members of the class could ask questions of the accused before they sat as the jury. I put my hand up to ask Ian if he had done it deliberately to be in court when the press was visiting. Before I was called on to speak Gina got in first. 'Chris, you are just a big show-off,' she said. 'You did all those things just to get your name in the paper!' Chris squirmed a bit and grinned but said nothing. Maybe not perfect court procedure but the magistrates decided that all the charges would be dismissed except the throwing of a chair because that could have hurt somebody.

The jury voted 'guilty' by 24 votes to one with two abstentions. I voted 'guilty.' The magistrates quickly agreed that the sentence should be to tidy the room after school for one week which Ian graciously accepted without argument. The men from the press then thanked everyone and said how impressive they had found the whole thing and that they hoped the 'story' would appear in the following Saturday's edition (it was then Wednesday). There was great excitement when the reporters said that they would ask the editor, Larry Lamb, if the Sun would pay for a coach to take the class to London the night before the story was run so that they could meet some of the staff and have the first 34 copies as they came off the printing press. 'Wow' was the general response. And they kept their word.

Of course, I had to get the acting head's permission to take the class to London late at night and by this time he knew about the visit. He was understandably annoyed that I had not told him about it. He felt he should have warned the local authority and the school governors and that they might have said 'no' - especially as the Sun had recently been bought from the Mirror Group by Rupert Murdoch and was getting a reputation for sensationalism and photographs of scantily clothed young women. 'Good thing I didn't tell you then!' I muttered into my beard. Actually, although he was a bit nervous about what might actually be printed he was also pleased that several parents had phoned him up to say how wonderful they thought the whole thing was. Several asked if they could come on the London trip.

We set off from school at about seven o'clock in the evening and were met at the Sun, still in Fleet Street in those days, by the Chief Sub-editor, known as the 'stone', who just by chance was the father of an old school-friend of mine. He took us to the office where 'our' reporter and photographer were based but they had been sent to Germany to cover an important international story. We then went to the outer office of the editor for bottles of lemonade, crisps and cakes –

Larry Lamb leaned around his door from an editor's meeting to say 'hallo – and sorry I am too busy to show you round myself. Great story though!'

After this we went to the chief-sub editor's office to watch the early edition of the paper being 'put to bed' some time just before midnight. We trooped to the press hall and having talked with a linotype operator watched the button being pushed to start the print run. This was very noisy and very exciting. The operator and the chief-sub both grabbed copies from the press as they whizzed past on their way to the bundling machines and out to the queue of waiting delivery vans. My friend's dad said 'You are on page 19 I'm afraid – opposite the pin-up on page 18. Never mind – front page next time!' He grabbed enough copies for everyone as the papers flew past. And there we were with two good sized photographs of the court in session. One picture was of the whole class with Chris in the dock listening to the charges being read, with me in the circle with my hand up waiting to speak – the other of the three magistrates looking very stern.

Underneath was a very friendly story with the headline –

'Pray silence for their worships Sally, David and Peter'

Chief magistrate David C called the chattering assembly to order – with a 2lb carpenter's hammer.

Clerk of the Peace Sally P shuffled her papers. The jury took their seats.....and the classroom court was in session.

Justice was being done at the G Secondary School, Aylesbury, Bucks.

Classmate Chris was in the dock. The defenders of form 2H had charged him with – Throwing chairs about.

Wrong doers appear before the jury of 12 year-olds every Friday.

Even form-teacher Derry Hannam, aged 30, has to ask to speak in the court.

His pupils have been known to suggest that his classroom court remarks were irrelevant.

Fair

The court is Mr Hannam's experiment to get his pupils to "reason for themselves and to be fair and just."

He said, "In the few months we have been doing this, we have noticed some marked change in some naturally anti-social aggressive children."

The court only comes into effect for misbehaviour between lessons.

Chris pleaded not guilty. He said he sometimes knocked his chair over for a bit of fun.

He was found guilty by 24 votes to one.

The sentence – an order to dust all the chairs and clean one desk twice a week for three weeks.

Chris didn't grumble. He said "It's fair and democratic."

And that's just the way Mr Hannam want his pupils to react.

Wow, was I relieved to read this? A not totally accurate piece of writing. I had never said that any kids in 2H were 'naturally anti-social aggressive children' for example or that the court only dealt with out of class issues. But really for a tabloid newspaper with a pretty poor image for sensationalism, it was not only fair but actually supportive of some progressive educational ideas! It had been worth explaining to the reporter on the way to his car that I had very serious citizenship, reasoning and communication purposes behind what we were doing and that the kids were at a young sub-adult stage where play was still an important way to learn. As they got older more accurately structured simulation might become more relevant but for now play still had its place.

He, or it might have been the photographer, had told me that his own kids were bored stiff at their secondary school and 'your kids are certainly not bored Derry - though they were taking it all very seriously.' I remember replying with 'Thanks – but of course children's play is a very serious matter to them. Adults sometimes forget that.' I hope I am not quite so pompous nowadays.

The acting head and the 2H parents were delighted and several wrote to me or phoned me up to tell me so. Some other staff became confirmed in their belief that I was some kind of hyper-ambitious self-publicist. More difficult to deal with though was the opinion of one of my own second-year humanities teachers, though it was said to my face and not behind my back fortunately. 'Don't you think it would have been fairer to take a few students from each of the second-year classes and not just keep it to your own class.'

She had a point, especially as we were working hard to create a democratic and sharing ethos across the whole year group. I said that the Sun had invited 2H as it was 'their story' and it would have been unfair to leave anyone from the class behind. This would have been necessary as it was hard enough weaving 34 kids through a working newspaper office. I wasn't totally comfortable with my answer though. There was a lesson for me in what she said. Perhaps I had not faced up to the reality of my larger responsibility. On the other hand, it was only my second year as a teacher.

That was not the end of the matter however. It had been noted at County Hall that one of their schools was in the national press and enquiries were made of the acting head. He told them that everything was under control, that he knew about it and was right behind the ideas – and further he was thinking of applying some of them across the whole school. By this stage, January of 1971, the second-year committee was beginning to work very well with three elected representatives from each of the seven classes. Just as the class courts, which operated in several classes now, dealt with issues within individual classrooms the second-year committee also sat as a court from time to time to deal with issues arising from the students' social use of the second-year part of the school building. I had argued with the head and the acting head that territory was important for young people and that if they had their own 'year space' which incorporated the various second year classrooms then the kids would be much more likely to look after it.

This proved to be the case and the second-year committee invited the acting head to one of its meetings to ask him if the year group could have access to their part of the building during morning and lunch breaks, which was at that time contrary to school policy. Partly it was able to do a deal with the acting head teacher because it has already secured the support and respect of the school caretaking team by the way it had cleaned and tidied the school hall after several lunchtime and evening discos; the first such school events to be organised by the students themselves. The quid pro quo offered by the committee was that they would take total responsibility for the care and sensible use the building.

The student organised discos had also generated a balance of cash with which the committee could offer a guarantee to make good any damage at no cost to the school budget. (The 2H treasurer and assistant treasurer, now with a year's experience of managing a bank account, trained a new team from the second- year committee and another account was opened at the bank where Andrew's dad was branch manager.) The acting head agreed to this new 'open-door' policy for break and lunchtime use for a trial period so long as there was no damage or vandalism, the prevention of which was the justification of the school policy. This really upset the students in other years who were only allowed inside at break time when it was raining. More muttering in the staffroom that 'Derry is trying to create his own bloody kingdom again.' But the fact was that only the second year had a year committee that on its own initiative could negotiate such a deal.

The acting head told the staff that he would happily cut a deal with any other year group if they got themselves organised and offered similar guarantees. Several parents phoned me to say how much they supported the idea and offered to help with any clubs or activities organized by the committee. Students in the fourth and fifth years rapidly organised their own committees as did the first year. The teacher responsible for the third year was vehemently opposed to this growth of student democracy and refused to assist his year group to hold elections until the acting head insisted that he should do so in preparation for the creation of the school council – of which more later.

A couple of weeks after the trip to the Sun the second-year committee had to deal with a case that tested its commitment. A door window had been broken by a second-year boy running through the corridor and banging on it. The committee asked the school caretaker how much it would cost to repair and he told them four pounds. They duly fined the student four pounds and gave him 20 weeks to pay it at 20p per week, having first paid the school the required sum from its bank account. He agreed and his parents were quite satisfied that he deserved the penalty. But – following our trip to the Sun somehow the Daily Mail got hold of the story of the broken window and without visiting the school wrote their article based on the Sun story. It was not quite so friendly though not actually hostile.

The Daily Mail wrote under the following headline –

"Child Judges Fine School Culprits," ...

"Classroom courts with children as judge and jury have fined four classmates for breaking windows at their school... the courts officially known as 'year committees' with two pupils from each class in the accused pupil's year, have the backing of Acting Headmaster Graham Stone (name changed). He said yesterday: 'The sentences are final although I am consulted about the decisions.' Severe. 'Pupils who do wrong accept the judgement. I find the children are far more logical in their conclusions and probably more fair in the long run .' But Mr Stone, 40, said the sentence on the window breakers was more severe than he would have passed. The boys would be able to pay the fine by instalment. An official of the Buckinghamshire education department said the school had launched an experiment in self-government. 'We are in favour of it. Naturally we are confident that the headmaster would not let it get out of hand.'"

I had no forewarning of the story, much of which was just made up by the anonymous journalist. There was only one year committee in the school and there was only one offender. I was very grateful for the support of the acting head, who actually had not been consulted over the particular financial penalty, though he knew that the second-year committee sometimes functioned as a court. The caretaker had told him that the kids had paid for the damage to the window and so he supported them continuing to have access to their spaces at break-times. Every caretaker in every school I have worked in has been willing to put themselves out to facilitate student-directed activities so long as what was going on was explained to them in advance. In fact, over the years I have generally found it easier to explain the idea of kids running things to caretakers than I did to some teachers! I never found out where the Mail got its information.

Worse was to come. A couple of days after the Mail story the supposedly up-market broadsheet The Daily Telegraph ran its own version, essentially lifted from the Mail, but under a headline that read "Kangeroo Courts sit in Aylesbury School." This time the writer, I suppose looking for a new angle, skewed the story to read as if kids were making decisions irresponsibly and beyond adult control. This 'Lord of the Flies' view of children very much fitted the political prejudices of the newspaper. Perhaps because it was almost entirely staffed by public schoolboys who had had any empathy they were born with destroyed by their schooling.

Fortunately, the issue died down, and as we had the full support of parents, acting head teacher, and local authority the unfairness of the tone of the reporting led nowhere. The kids were disgusted of course. I doubt if any of them have ever bought a copy of the Daily Telegraph during their lives! The second-year committee wrote a long letter to the Telegraph explaining how they worked and complaining about the unjust and inaccurate tone of the report. It was not published of course. They never received a reply. There was some useful learning about media for the students and I also learned to make sure that I had the maximum possible control over press coverage of student democracy in action in future.

The story did cause a frisson of anxiety at County Offices however and an assistant director of education was sent down to the school to find out what actually was going on. It was possibly not an accident that this person was Tim Brighouse, many years later knighted for his work in raising standards in London's schools through collaboration rather than competition. He seemed delighted by what I was doing. He had heard something about it from his wife who was a teacher at the school.

I was very encouraged by his comment that 'when I'm a director of education somewhere I'm going to appoint you to a headship.' He didn't – but our paths have crossed several times since and we have reminisced about some of the kids in 2H. It did lead to several evenings at his house though with outline plans spread on the floor of a major new campus school to be built at the large new 'city' of Milton Keynes. We talked about the importance of student democracy and I emphasised my view of the need for groups of kids to have control of a part of the school that they could feel was their territory. Then they would take responsibility for it. Preferably a village-like collection of buildings. I like to think that these discussions had some effect of the final design of the school which became Stantonbury Campus with 'carpets and Christian names Derry' Geoff Cooksey as its first director (Moon, 1983).

So why did the newspapers only really show interest in the class and year courts and largely ignore the more important and much more time consuming but purposeful class and year committee meetings? Why was justice sexier than democracy? It can't have just been the opportunity to portray what was happening as 'loony left teachers giving irresponsible kids irresponsible power.' The tabloid Sun had every opportunity to do this and it chose not to. In fact, it was the most accurate of the three reports. The mid-range Mail was also broadly responsible. It was the broadsheet up-market Telegraph that corrupted the story without regard for what harm it might do. Could it be that all the children of Sun readers would be in state schools whereas a large proportion of Telegraph parents would have their children in private schools and thus relish stories that reassured them that their money was being well-spent?

I decided that in future I would feed stories to the local press which, I soon learned, love to print material with long lists of kid's names in them so that each member of the family and friends will buy a copy of the paper. This makes the paper disposed to write good things about a school and to avoid negative stories because they don't want to lose a source of pre-written articles that have a circulation value. They are always short of staff and run on a shoestring so given a chance to save journalist time they can nearly always be tempted to allow themselves to be spoon-fed. This policy has worked very well for me ever since, especially a few years later when I was a school manager.

Exposure to the national press had a somewhat inflationary effect on the self-importance of the students of 2H. When the local Bucks Advertiser picked up on the story from the Sun it asked if a reporter and a photographer could attend a meeting and a sitting of the class court. One boy, David B, opined that they are '...only the local paper so we shouldn't put ourselves out too much.'

Chapter 9 – 2H Teaches the teachers

It was around this time that a group of student teachers visited the class with their tutors. The acting head, Graham, was bringing them to our 2H classroom at the same time that school reception summoned me to meet them. We took different routes and the visitors arrived at the class in my absence. The kids had got the room into its circular configuration for a meeting with the visitors and following introductions from Graham had started to explain their system of self-government. I was told afterwards by one of the tutors that Andrew once again explained that 'Mr Hannam is a bit soft so if we didn't govern ourselves it would be chaos in here.'

Fifty years later Andrew, himself now retired as a deputy head teacher with a strong commitment to student democracy and student voice, tells me that he remembers these incidents vividly and with much embarrassment. Actually, they made me laugh for weeks at the time, and still do. They seemed to vindicate exactly what I was trying to achieve. Power and responsibility were indeed being shared and the rule of law was not solely dependent on the technical authority of the adult. Authority belonged to the collective within a framework of democracy and human rights and was respected because of it. It reminded me of the story that A.S. Neill used to tell about a student at Summerhill who asked another older kid 'who is that old bloke who hangs around the school all the time?' 'Oh that's only Neill – he's the head teacher or something.'

Following this visit, one of the teachers' college tutors, who was head of the philosophy of education course and a secret admirer of Neill and Summerhill, invited me and 2H to deliver a seminar on 'Shared Responsibility" for the final year student teachers at Westminster College, Oxford. Another trip! The meeting decided unanimously that they wanted to go especially when they learned that the college was in Oxford and that they would get a free coach ride and an afternoon out of school. The enthusiasm rose further when Sharon announced that her mum used to work as a cleaner at an Oxford college and '...you get lots of leftover cake to eat.'

I kept quiet about the fact that this was a lowly teacher training college. The meeting discussed how to organise the presentation. It was decided that I would give an introduction 'to get them to listen' and then the ten students who wanted to give speeches would do so followed by questions that anyone in the class could answer. That included me, though I was instructed not to answer every question myself unless nobody else wanted to say anything. I had another laugh about the idea that the only point of my speech was 'to get them to listen.' The reality was that the student teachers were so amazed that twelve-year-olds could 'give speeches' that they got far more instant and total attention than I did!

I still have the notes for my introduction and summaries of most of the kids' speeches. Their plan was superb. I was to explain why I allowed the class to develop its 'system' and then they would explain the jobs that emerged. Each student would talk about their job in the order that they were created. The form captains gave a joint talk that they had written together about the fact that they were elected for half a term and that they could not be re-elected immediately if there was someone else who wanted the job who had not had the chance to do it previously. (1H/2H class law number 6!) They described their duties, including taking it in turns to chair the class meeting and supervise the discussion and the voting. They explained how important it was to allow everyone a fair turn at speaking when chairing a meeting and that it had been 'scary' at first but 'you soon get used to it.' The class secretary then explained how important it was to have a record of every meeting and that he kept getting re-elected as he was so good at it. He had brought photocopies of the minutes of a meeting for everyone to see.

The treasurers talked about the importance of looking after the class funds and the class taxes properly (everyone paid a penny a week unless they couldn't afford it) and that they had a proper bank account 'because one of our dads is a bank manager.' Organisers of the class drama club, chess club, fashion show, football club, class parties and discos committee, all said their pieces as did several editors of parts of the class newspaper. The class representatives on the second-year committee talked about their work and how 'our ideas are spreading through all the second-year classes.' Steven D wound up with a description of our visit to the Sun newspaper. I was incredibly proud of them all and it was very well received by the audience. 'I thought they would never stop clapping,' said Jenny B afterwards.

My talk was a fairly pompous though heartfelt comment on the 'state of the planet' that we were leaving to our children. Nuclear testing in the atmosphere had only recently ceased and one of my own children had a birth defect that was probably associated with radiation effects. I pontificated that it was important not to fill children's heads with vast packets of 'facts' that we adults thought important but to give them the freedom to follow their own interests wherever and as far as they led within a framework of core ideas, concepts and skills. We should '...foster the individual and collaborative skills, the creativity and ability to play, passion and self-confidence of our children in communities of concern and mutual respect where they learn to care for and nurture the well-being of each other.'

The class sat patiently hoping I would soon finish and the audience appeared to be politely engaged. Then came the kids turn and the audience collectively sat up in their seats. The questions went on for a long time and about 20 of the student teachers said they would like to see the class in action. It was a memorable event and led to several more 'lecturing' visits to the college. The student teachers visited 2H in groups over several weeks. The tutor who had invited us wrote saying 'Thank you so much for coming. The students are buzzing with talk about it. The visit was both educational and therapeutic – for students – and for me!....and by the way the 'correct vogue' word for play, the importance of which I entirely agree, is 'simulation.'

Well actually I didn't agree that play and simulation are the same thing at all, but it was an encouraging response and once again led to some nice comments from parents. One wrote to me to say that 'Peter is only 12 years old yet he is much more confident at speaking in front of others than I am. I run a chain of shoe shops and this is a quality I look for in new staff and find it quite rare – especially in young people. In my opinion you are making these kids employable!! Thank you.'

Chapter 10 – Democracy begins to Impact on the Whole School – The School Council

After the first term of the second year I was given another financial promotion which clarified my role as head of second-year as well as team leader of the second-year humanities team. This time my immediate boss, the head of lower school, was properly consulted. His status was not at all threatened as I was nominally also his assistant. There were no problems within the humanities staff but much more muttering about my undue influence from certain sections of the staff room.

These were compounded when Graham, the acting head teacher, told me that he planned to create a school council around the work I was doing in the lower school and that he wanted me to set it up. I was to be the chair and I would receive another small financial promotion. (Actually these 'small' financial lifts did not seem so little to me as I had just bought a larger house and our third child had just arrived!) Graham announced that he intended to seek a headship in another school at the end of the year when the head returned so that he could develop these ideas in a whole school. We began a series of visits to other schools in the South Midlands that had up and running school councils.

One trip was to a girls' school about 20 miles away. It was quite a big school with about a thousand students. The school council met in the school gym. The council included two or three students from every class, teachers from each year group, a representative of the catering staff and the school caretaker. It was chaired by the head teacher and all the students from a year group attended on a rotational basis so that during the course of a year every student and every adult in the school had an opportunity to see the council in action. It met three times per term, nine times a year, and the head teacher chose the agenda items from suggestions from both students and staff.

The school was in a middle-class area and the meeting was very polite and orderly but for me a bit too contrived and lacking in the energy and spontaneity of a genuinely student-controlled event. Graham was very taken with this model though and said 'this is how we are going to do it Derry - but I want you to chair the meetings. I want to attend though.' I didn't argue too much as it seemed to me to be an amazing opportunity in my second year of teaching. I was beginning to learn how some of the teachers might react though, and I suggested that maybe the post should be advertised and I would be sure to apply. This was firmly vetoed. 'I'm in charge and I make the decisions,' he said, 'and they'll just have to live with it if they don't like it.' Not quite what I was hoping to hear! He was planning to leave at the end of the year and would not have to live with the consequences if it all went very wrong. I, at this stage, was not planning to move to another school – though thanks to an offer too good to refuse, I did!

One trip to learn about democratic experiments in other schools was organised by a member of the second-year humanities team. We went to the recently opened Countesthorpe College in Leicestershire. Graham did not want to come. The school was the brainchild of the innovative comprehensive school pioneer Tim McMullen. It was a 'bridge too far' for Graham but he allowed the whole second-year team to make the visit without him. It had its funny side.

All seven of us squeezed into my Land Rover which had a broken fuel gauge at the time. We ran out of diesel about half-way. A passing farmer stopped to help. He had a gallon of paraffin which he offered to sell – 'it will get you to the next garage,' he advised. It did – but only just. We passed a United States Air Force base just as two F4 Phantoms were roaring down the runway with their afterburners full on producing large clouds of black smoke as they went into a 45-degree climb. That was nothing compared to the smoke that was coming out of my Land Rover along with the stink of the illegal half burned fuel! We made it though, without having the vehicle impounded and had an interesting visit.

Had we arrived five years later we would have seen an extraordinary experiment in school democracy and curriculum innovation for a UK state school (Watts, 1977). As it was, we saw a building site with many younger children that the community college had never planned to provide for. The staff were struggling with mud and temporary buildings. We liked the idea of learning 'pods' for the younger students but we were not terribly impressed by the quality of the teaching materials which looked like endless piles of not very attractive worksheets. It seemed to us that although the curriculum organisation was unusual for the younger children with headings such as 'the individual and the group - IG' there was actually little scope for student directed or collaborative learning. The students we spoke to liked the informal atmosphere with staff who were known by their first names, and there was no school uniform, but they did not seem to be as motivated to learn as our kids were.

What was amazingly different was the approach to school governance. This was based on the 'moot'; an assembly which seemed to be meeting weekly at the time of our visit and appeared to be open to all staff and older students only. We did not see a meeting in progress but received rather mixed messages from students. Many said that they rarely if ever attended because the teachers talked all the time. The teachers we spoke to were very positive about the moot however. Some said it was what had attracted them to work in the school. When pressed, several did say that some of their colleagues did talk a great deal and tended to use language that was alien and incomprehensible to the students.

The Warden was ill on the day of our visit and we were shown round by an IG teacher. He explained that Tim did not regard himself as a 'Head Teacher' but rather as chief executive whose job was to implement the decisions of the moot, even if he personally disagreed with them. We were given a statement of his philosophy and aims and I was very impressed by his revolutionary vision and willingness to share power with both staff and students.

The big question in my mind as we left was how was the warden going to sell this vision to the local people of Countesthorpe and Blaby. It was apparent from newspaper cuttings on a noticeboard that the school was already having difficulties with the local press and Conservative member of parliament. This was not a secondary modern school. The Countesthorpe parents, unlike ours, were not particularly interested in teachers as people who would rebuild the damaged self-confidence caused by failure in the selection process. This was a comprehensive school that would inevitably have a proportion of parents with high traditional academic aspirations for their children. They might not wish to be part of the 'educational revolution'. They might look for traditional hierarchical authority to achieve their goals.

From our brief visit we did not get the impression that the school was putting as much effort into winning over the local community as it should for its own good. It was spending too much time and energy in debating internally with itself. No doubt the ill-health of the Warden was not helping.

The bad press that the school was beginning to receive was to build to a crescendo over the next three years before subsiding for a while and then returning with a vengeance some years later. Finally, an enquiry forced the resignation of the then Warden, John Watts. This despite the fact that the school had achieved international acclaim and was actually achieving very good academic results.

I recall the conversation on the journey home. The visit caused us to reflect on exactly what we were asking of children and staff in our own 'experiment.' None of us had been trained in any way to teach 'integrated humanities with a strong emphasis on self-directed learning in a democratic framework.' We were indeed making it up as we went along. We began to realize that we were asking children to function in ways and spaces that were traditionally the preserve of adults. These demands involved curriculum and behaviour decisions around the creation and enforcement of rules, semi-formal class and year committee processes, and negotiations with authority.

We had created the spaces for the learning to happen experientially and it was obviously working. On the other hand, we were expecting of ourselves as teachers a new willingness to share 'our' spaces and responsibilities with young students. We were learning to listen and respond to them and their ideas and to actually encourage them to move into what were traditionally adult preserves. We were creating new environments where students and staff, young people and adults, collaborated as human beings of equal value. At times the students were showing that they could become independent from the adults altogether and 'do it for themselves' – and we were, so far at least, getting away with it!

We had, miraculously it now seems, the support of parents, the head and acting head teachers and two other newly appointed assistant heads. One of these had experience of counseling and some psychological training. She was immediately sympathetic to our democratic listening approach and especially to children with historical behavioral difficulties. The other had come from a school in Jersey that was developing an IDE (inter-disciplinary enquiry) approach to curriculum who absolutely supported what we were doing. He talked of demolishing walls on the second-year corridor so that we could work more closely as teams in shared spaces. The head teacher of his previous school had been the same John Watts who was to take over Countesthorpe College when Tim McMullen retired due to ill-health in 1972.

The whole team, especially those with the more 'difficult' classes, were very keen on this idea of creating an open plan space where the influence of the more experienced teachers could support them in creating the kind of relationships that they wanted to have with the students. Also it would enable teachers to work with individuals and small groups leaving other adults always around. Though it was a challenge to wonder how well students would manage a 'quiet time' in a space containing over 200 young people! These building plans never materialised at this school though I was to move on to a brand-new school in neighbouring Oxfordshire where the Humanities Department was designed in precisely this way - with large and small spaces, a film projection/lecture theatre, recording studios, art and craft bays and its own library. That is another book!

I realised just what generosity of spirit was coming from the more experienced members of the team. It was easy for me – I was a beginner, albeit a year or two older than the average, with no experience of or conditioning by traditional hierarchical authoritarian school regimes. I also had a firm, though not fully articulated, commitment to releasing the creativity, imagination and natural conviviality of children. This required an environment where they could learn experientially how to share responsibility for the creation and maintenance of a community. I was lucky to work with a group of six teachers who very largely shared these aims and values. We also had the support of the parents and, through sheer chance, of part of the press – national as well as local!

We were causing dissension in the staff room however. It had been noticed that the second-year humanities team were hardly ever seen in it. Most of our breaks and lunchtimes were spent in activities with our own or each other's classes or students. A massive amount of learning was going on within the second-year team that was having some effect on the first-year team. It also had some spin-off for the teachers who taught other non-humanities subjects to the second-year classes, though not all were sympathetic or supportive.

A major plus was the fact that the art and drama departments had to all extents and purposes joined the team. The heads of both departments became excited by the volume and quality of the creative writing, especially poetry, that was coming from the second-year students and often used it as stimulus for their lessons. They also noted and enjoyed a more forthcoming and 'willing to participate' attitude in many of the students especially a concern for and interest in each other's ideas. The second-year kids actually formed their own drama club for which some had begun to write their own plays. It was the students who invited the very popular drama teacher to work with their club rather than the other way around.

A number of senior heads of department did not share these perceptions however, and nor did some of their junior colleagues. Belatedly I began to realise that I had not thought through what the impact of what we were doing would be on those who were not a part of it. On the other hand, I was only in my second year of teaching and I had never been on a course on 'how to manage change.' At the time I thought that it was the responsibility of senior management to worry about the effects we were having on other staff power bases in the school I! I still do.

By this time our team was beginning to get on well with, and build bridges to, the humanities team that was working with the older years 10 and 11 students (aged 14-16). Theirs was pioneering work for this age group. In the time normally allowed for history and geography they had created a thematic social studies course grounded in topics likely to be of concern and interest to adolescents. It was entirely coursework assessed and generally popular with the students.

The timetable did not allow any overlap of staffing with the lower school's humanities teams so the two teaching teams never met in any formal way. In hindsight this seems a strange way to go about things, but once created separate 'fiefdoms/curriculum power bases' rarely come together organically in secondary schools. Nonetheless I was getting to know and like the two key co-creators of the upper school humanities course and they in turn were taking an interest in the democratic and curriculum developments emerging in the second year.

We had begun to talk about how to bridge what was happening in the second year with their courses. We could see that control of the third-year curriculum would become a struggle for power between lower and upper school humanities teams on the one hand and the traditional departments of English, history, geography and religious studies on the other unless the ground was carefully prepared in advance. I do not believe that Graham, the acting head, was deep down an authoritarian by nature but both he and the head teacher were prepared, if they really wanted something to happen, to use authority to limit discussion and impose a decision.

Their reasoning was that if you had the luxury of appointing all the staff for a new school, such as Countesthorpe, then staff democracy would be manageable but that that was not the case at our school and that unless decisive steps were taken change would never come. They were probably right. It is a dilemma that faces anyone who wants to change an organisation from above. We were all making it up as we went along – including the head who was on secondment, the acting head and the senior managers. With hindsight we should probably all have been more careful.

Graham decided that he was not impressed with the Countesthorpe approach to school democracy. He was certainly not going to be a chief executive answerable to any school moot or parliament. Without further discussion he devised a constitution for the school council and appointed another young teacher to assist me and act as secretary. He did not want elected pupils to play these roles. By this time, I was fairly certain that he was not intending to stay at the school for another year. 'Well, it's not how I would want it but let's give it a try and see what happens,' I thought.

Every year was to be encouraged to elect year committees following the example of the second year with two representatives from each of the seven forms. All were to attend school council meetings with eight students coming from the sixth form of 16-18 year-olds. Teachers were to be represented from each department plus every head of year. Every group of non-teaching staff such as kitchen and caretaking were also represented. It was to be a vast body, quite different to anything we had created so far. Nearly a hundred students and as many as thirty adults. In addition half-year groups of about a hundred and twenty students were to attend in rotation as observers.

The agenda was to be constructed from suggestions from each year group for students and through departmental representatives for staff. Graham as acting head would have a right of veto and the agenda would be published on the day before the meeting. Meetings were to be monthly followed by a feedback staff meeting. Student representatives would feed back to their year committees and registration classes. The first of the four meetings that actually took place was in February of my second academic year at the school.

I was very nervous and also very naive. Apart from the 1H/2H/second-year project, which had started in one class and moved fairly organically into the whole year group, this was a top-down imposition on the rest of the school. The constitution was explained by Graham to a senior staff meeting of heads of year and heads of department. On the whole the heads of year were pleased by the development and were happy to create elected year committees. Several senior heads of department were critical of various details which seemed to be a cover for deeper hostility but no negative proposals were made. The reaction of the rest of the staff was much more divided.

The humanities teams were all in favour and especially the second-year team. A caucus of serious opposition emerged from other departments though and a special 'protest' staff meeting was called to object to the lack of discussion with staff about the creation of the council. This meeting was attended by twelve junior staff and several heads of department but boycotted by the humanities teams. Objections emerged and were minuted about the way in which the school council was being created, the failure to have a staff meeting before each council meeting, and to the fact that the chair and secretary had only been in the school a short time and lacked appropriate experience.

I did not attend the meeting but was told afterwards by supportive people that the whole point of the meeting was to make my role impossible. A delegation approached me the next day to put it to me that the secretary and I should resign from our council positions unless Graham, the acting head teacher, gave way. We both refused. A letter was sent to Graham setting out these points with some teachers threatening to refuse to let students leave their lessons to attend council meetings unless their demands were met.

Graham's response was immediate and forthright. He called a staff meeting at which he rejected any discussion of his plans and threatened any staff inclined to sabotage a school council meeting by withholding students with a disciplinary hearing before the school governors. The council secretary and I felt quite uncomfortable and wondered how a democratic council could function in such an authoritarian atmosphere. On the other hand, waiting for all the opposition to soften and give the project a chance to succeed could take a long time and Graham did not have a long time – I learned he had secretly been appointed to the headship of a new school and was planning to leave at the end of the school year on the return of the real head teacher. I began to wonder if perhaps I should do the same as the situation was becoming too complicated and I was beginning to feel used and a long way out of my comfort zone!

Despite the political staff room pressures that I was feeling the second-year students were excited about the new school council forum as they knew that they were the only year that already had a democratic structure. There were discussions in each class to decide what issues should be put on the first school council agenda. There were some proposals relating to school dances, better facilities for storing bicycles and one relating to procedure.

The second-year committee had learned from experience not to make a decision on an important issue at the first meeting at which it was discussed. The class representatives would always take the proposed decision or options back to their classes for further discussion and then make the final decision at the next meeting of the second-year committee. They proposed that the school council should work in the same way. I think that they had no other proposals for the school council because they were content with the freedoms and privileges they had already negotiated with Graham, the acting head teacher. The big issue for other years was the opening of the school at break times but of course the second years had already achieved this for their year as far as their corridor and suite of rooms was concerned. They also had their own democratic forum at which second-year issues could be resolved.

All the other heads of year had elections in their constituent classes and there was a palpable air of democratic interest and excitement throughout the entire student body in the run up to the first meeting.

The first agenda was largely uncontroversial consisting of items concerning the details of the school uniform and, as expected, the reopening of the whole school at lunchtimes following the closure two years previously due to unresolved vandalism. Given the size of the council the first meeting went smoothly though there were staff questions about the non-elected role of chair and secretary. Graham stated that this was his decision and that he had chosen the 'best people for the jobs.' That was not universally well received by all the staff representatives. But they did not persist. I said, perhaps unwisely, that I hoped the posts would be elected before too long. Graham made it clear by facial expression that I should keep my opinion to myself on this issue. With hindsight I can see that it is possible that he felt that he could easily keep control with two young teachers running the school council. I do not know for sure and I have never had the opportunity of discussing it with him. Various sub-committees were created. Many procedural issues were resolved. The meeting lasted for an hour and the secretary had minutes published within a couple of days.

The second meeting also went well with sensible recommendations and decisions being made around improvements to footpaths, bicycle racks, changing rooms, school dances, and fire extinguishers.

It was not until the third meeting that we hit trouble. I had been a little disappointed that nothing controversial had been discussed at the first two meetings and that votes were tending to be unanimous. I felt that little was being learned about how to listen to alternative points of view and to compromise as had certainly been the case in the 1H/2H class meetings and the second-year committee meetings. On the other hand, I was pleased that we had made it to the third meeting without a crisis.

This third meeting took place in early May of my second year at the school. The agenda was largely as before with items about dinner menus, school magazines and girl's uniform, but along with these fairly mundane items Graham allowed two others onto the agenda that promised a livelier debate.

One was from the second-year committee. In the humanities lessons the students came into the working spaces or classrooms whether the staff were there or not and got to work on their projects, or organising the room for a meeting. In other lessons they had to wait outside the room until the teacher arrived. Some teachers were regularly late for lessons. The second years wanted to bring this up at the school council to request that all teachers should allow students into the classroom when the teacher was late. By this time the fourth-year committee had begun to function well and they in their turn wanted to discuss delays in staff returning marked humanities work. They felt that in some cases it took so long to be returned that they had forgotten what it was about. Graham, slightly to my surprise, allowed these two items onto the agenda. With more experience I might have questioned his judgement.

The council duly assembled for its third meeting. Before we could start on the agenda a very angry staff representative from one of the two principle teacher unions in the school demanded to be heard on a point of order. He insisted that items concerning staff conduct should be removed from the agenda immediately. It sounded like a prepared speech over which a lot of care had been taken and which probably represented considerable discussion at a union meeting to which I had not been invited, even though I was a member.

'Teachers have a code of professional conduct which would not permit them to discuss or criticise other teachers in the presence of pupils.' This put me on the spot. I looked to Graham for guidance but he said nothing. I wondered if he was expecting it. I thought 'well I will let the council listen to the argument and make the decision.' I invited comments on what had been said. There was a stony silence. So, I put the speech to the vote as if it had been a proposal like any other. It was agreed without dissent. I wondered what would have happened if some confident second-year student had said 'If it is OK to talk about student behaviour in general in school council why can't we talk about teacher behaviour in general.' But no-one did! There may well have been a walk-out of some if not all of the teaching staff representatives had any such discussion taken place.

The meeting continued reasonably well though there was a change in the atmosphere. A certain anxiety had crept into the proceedings and I think the students were much more cautious about what they said for the rest of the meeting, but recommendations from the uniform and dance sub-committees were, nonetheless, heard and agreed.

The issue of the discussion of staff in the presence of students was not over however. I was summoned to a meeting of the union of which I was a member. It was firmly put to me that my behaviour in being willing to chair a meeting where such items were to be discussed was unprofessional. I thought for a minute about using the defence that the acting head teacher had allowed these items onto the agenda, but I decided that that would be ducking the issue so I just resigned from that union and applied to join the other. I had left the school before my application was considered.

By the time of the fourth meeting I was working my notice as was Graham. From the agenda and minutes, it is clear that it was another uncontroversial affair though a great deal of business was dealt with and the discussion had begun to move beyond uniform and changing rooms to rearrangements of the school day to allow an afternoon break. The size of the meetings had proved to be manageable but it was clear that only the more articulate and confident students were getting a chance to speak.

Was the union right to veto items concerning staff behaviour? Was I naive? Was Graham wrong to allow the items onto the agenda in the first place? Should I have stopped the second- year committee from bringing forward the question of late arrival of staff at lessons?

It turned out that the fourth-year question about the delayed and late return of marked work had a perfectly rational and acceptable explanation. The teachers involved had been quite content to explain the reason at the council meeting. It concerned the need of the examination authority to see some of the students' coursework as part of the assessment process. There was no reason at all why this could not have been discussed. It would have helped the students to understand the procedure to which the staff had to adhere.

The late arrival of second-year teachers would have been a more difficult issue for open discussion and perhaps with hindsight I should have told the second-year committee that I would quietly raise their concerns with the teachers themselves. Some individual students had attempted to discuss the issue with the worst offending teachers but had been told that they were being rude in questioning teacher behaviour. Some of the second-year council members felt that they had done something wrong in raising the issue at the school council. I reassured them that it was my responsibility in allowing the item to go forward. I think that they were happy with that. Others felt the outcome was unfair. Of course, they were right, but you have to work with the realities of every situation and compromise is sometimes required.

The personal hostility that had emerged around the creation of the council had begun to make me feel that although the school had moved much faster towards democracy that I could have ever hoped, with committees working well in every year and the sixth-form, nonetheless my own role was becoming too intense for my own good. After all, I was still a normal class teacher with a full workload and no extra time for my new whole school responsibilities. Graham let me know privately and under oath of secrecy that he had accepted a headship in another school. That made me feel even more insecure as I had no idea what the reaction of the returning head would be to the way in which Graham had set about introducing change.

The returning head had supported me in my first year before his secondment but to continue doing so might be much more difficult for him. The arguments at the third council meeting clinched it for me and I accepted an invitation to apply for the post of head of the humanities department at a very large new school in a neighbouring county. The opportunity to participate in appointing my own team and the provision of a brand-new purpose-built humanities building designed to facilitate team-teaching and collaborative learning were too good to miss.

The thought of no longer working with 1H/2H made me a little sad but as there were no plans to extend the humanities programme into the third-year this would have not been possible even if I stayed at the school, though perhaps I could have continued to be their form teacher.

All this after just two years as a teacher. It had been quite a ride! Graham and I resigned on the same day and both of us gradually got absorbed in the needs of our new posts.

Chapter 11 – Jo's Story

Through my last half-term at the school class 2H and the second year as a whole had become more and more mature. Year committee meetings happened whether I attended or not. The second-year humanities team ran itself, with more collaborative team teaching happening all the time. There were regular Friday morning talks by visitors, or the staff team, with students able to choose which one they would go to. Within 2H itself the quality of the community and the maturity of its capacity to organise itself for the benefit both of the whole class and for occasionally unhappy individual students was extraordinary. I have reams of notes that are moving to read after 50 years but I will close my account with one particular incident that encapsulates everything about their capacity for generosity and kindness.

A girl, Jo, had joined the class at the end of the first term of the second year. She was from a travelling Romany family and her father was in prison for a long sentence. It was agreed that she should join my second-year humanities class. She had had many difficulties in her previous schools and she quickly made friends with some much older rather disturbed and anti-social students. She then began to pick fights with members of the class and call in the support of her older friends when the bullying was resisted. She quickly appeared before the class court which she laughed at and at first refused to accept its decisions. She was shaken by the fact that the whole class stood up to her and had no hesitation in calling on adult support to challenge her behaviour.

On one occasion two of her fourth-year bully friends were summoned to appear before the 2H class court. At first, they refused saying that they were not going to accept having to explain themselves to younger kids. They were shocked when their head of their year told them that unless they agreed to appear before the 2H court their parents would be told and that in the last resort they would be excluded from school for a week by him because of their bullying behaviour. The choice was theirs. Come to the 2H court and accept its verdict or parents called in with exclusion to follow.

I was extraordinarily grateful for this close support and confidence in student democracy shown by a much older colleague who at one point had been opposed to the whole idea. Graham also had heard about the problem and let me know that if the head of the fourth-year had not supported me he would have done. Two very subdued fourth-year girls and Jo duly appeared before the 2H court charged with bullying two rather vulnerable class members who had nonetheless stood up to them and used the class justice process with confidence. They were found guilty after offering a very incoherent defence that the class members had sworn at them. Nobody believed them. Their confidence melted away under determined questioning from the magistrates and members of the class/jury. Eventually they volunteered an apology. Jo herself began to cry.

The punishment was so simple. The older girls were told to stop bullying younger kids and the magistrates would write a letter to their head of year telling him of the decision. They said that the shame of having to appear before a court of younger kids would probably stop them plus the threat of being reported to their head of year as persistent bullies if it happened again. It was a brilliant example of younger kids having a forum for dealing with bullying so that they were empowered to act – so empowered in fact that the solution could show some respect for the dignity of the bullies so long as they stopped their bullying.

Jo herself was told that she had to write a one-page article for the class newspaper called 'Why people bully other people.' The court as always was on a Friday and on Monday the magistrates were waiting to read Jo's article. But she did not come to school. One of the girls in the class said that she would call at Jo's house to see if she was ill or truanting. Jo's mother told her that Jo was afraid to come to school because she would be bullied by the class and that she as parent was going to complain to the acting head about it.

What happened next was quite extraordinary. The students of 2H realised that there was a real possibility that Jo would be excluded permanently if she did not change her behaviour. Without telling me, the form captains called a class meeting after school for anyone from the class who wanted to attend to discuss what could be done to help Jo. I found out about the meeting almost by accident and was told that 'you can come if you want to.' They cared about Jo and realised that she was very unhappy. They were determined that they should be allowed to try to find their own solution.

Eighteen members of the class turned up – nearly all those who did not need to catch school buses to get home. It was run as a normal class meeting and many ideas were suggested. Robert proposed that the class should be kind to Jo on three days a week and not speak to her on the other two to see on which days she behaved in a kind way to others. This idea was firmly rejected as unkind. Sharon's solution, which was adopted, was rather more humane and, considering that she herself had been bullied by Jo, quite remarkable. Sharon proposed that Jo should be elected to be a form captain in a 'rigged' election to show that everyone respected her and wanted to give her the opportunity to show that she could be responsible. At this point David said that he wanted to resign as one of the class magistrates so that Jo could be elected in his place. He argued that it would help Jo if she had to decide what to do when other people broke the class laws.

Jo reappeared the next day and as planned an emergency class meeting was held at which one of the form captains and one of the magistrates duly resigned. There was an immediate election at which Jo was proposed and seconded and nobody stood against her. She was unanimously elected with no one against and no abstentions. Jo burst into tears and ran out of the room. I nearly cried as well. I followed her out of the room and brought her back in. It took her several minutes to bring herself to accept – to be able to accept the care and concern, love even, of her class. In accepting the roles she said '...nobody has ever been kind to me in school...ever! Thank you.'

In fact, she did the jobs really well. The following day the required article about bullying appeared on the class newspaper wall. It was three pages long not one. It was the longest piece of writing that Jo had ever done.

Sadly, her family moved on yet again before the end of the term. Had she stayed at the school she would almost certainly have been re-elected. She never bullied anyone in the class again and no more was seen of her older 'friends.'

The action of the class over the Jo incident had an indelible effect on me. The ex-students with whom I am in contact over forty years later remember it vividly. It was a solution that no adult could ever have contrived. It was a moral act of a high order. Lawrence Kohlberg (1987) would have instantly recognized the learning that must have occurred over the previous terms that the class had been together that allowed such morally mature actions to be possible. It did not happen by chance. It was nurtured in an empowered democratic environment in which thirty-four young people had had the opportunity to learn experientially how to take responsibility for themselves and each other. Above all they had learned to have empathy and that kindness was not the same as weakness. It justified the whole project beyond my wildest dreams and it still reduces me to tears just thinking and writing about it.

PART THREE –

WHAT WAS IT ALL ABOUT AND WHAT HAS IT GOT TO DO WITH NOW?

Chapter 12 – Love and the Public Service Ethic

Although my teaching practices during teacher training and my first two years of teaching substantially involved 'making it up as we went along' there were nonetheless some clear guiding principles at work. I will try to identify these and attempt to give them some solid theoretical support.

But first perhaps it should be said that this story is really about love and kindness. The principle that motivates many people who work in education and health and used to be known as the 'public service ethic'. To work for the 'greater good of all.' A source of human motivation forgotten or never understood by the neo-liberal minded privatisers who have seen so much of our public sector as a milch cow to be squeezed for profit. They move in and contaminate the ground that this book is all about by measuring what can easily be measured and putting a price on what can easily be costed while ignoring or never beginning to understand what is the heart of the matter. The growing number of cases of corruption, nepotism and payment of absurdly high salaries to chief executive head teachers of multi-academy trusts are clear examples of this in the privatisation of the English state school system.

I realise that there is a danger that this can sound like those dreadfully trite tautologous 'mystical wise words' that people fire around on Facebook and that this could prevent what I want to say being taken seriously. I must take that chance because at the heart of my work was love of the imaginations of children and the way that they play and create. A deep belief that children are people who deserve respect and whose experiences, both good and bad, should be taken seriously. People who by the age of eleven have already learned a great deal and whose knowledge and interests deserve our respect as teachers not to be brushed aside as irrelevant to the greater purpose of the prescribed subject, school or national curriculum and their associated test results and attainment. People who have a natural curiosity and capacity to learn that it is the task of the teacher to nurture not to obstruct. People who learn best from and with others and not as isolated individuals to be set competitively against each other to see who can get the highest score in tests that exist for the greater glory of the school, the government, or the big education companies who write and profit from them.

Government all too frequently surrenders to the smooth statistical salesmanship of the 'testocracy' with its generously funded expense account lobbyists. Politicians buy into its pseudo-scientific sounding, but ultimately devoid of meaning, grades and numbers in the hope that that is where the votes lie. Never mind the collateral damage done to their victims. Government then pays again for the 'big data' peddled by the testocrats to argue that the schools and their idle teachers are failing - or sometimes the opposite. They want us to believe that their latest test for ever younger children or their latest 'rigorous' toughening of examination courses is leading to 'world-class' improvements. Sometimes they argue for both failure (the teachers) and success (the politicians and testocrats) at the same time! I have come to hate this testocratic world and to despise its willingness to destroy both childhood and the professional identity and autonomy of teachers.

I love the attitude of the Finns to the international testocracy of PISA (OECD 2009). Finland was both shocked and mildly amused when its education system emerged as the 'best in Europe' in the first round of PISA testing and reformers from all over the world began to descend upon their country. The Finns themselves knew all too well of the weaknesses of their system and its failure as yet to break the world wide phenomenon of the link between parental wealth and school learning - though they are making better progress than any other country in the challenging journey to genuine equality of opportunity.

The attitude of Finland's minister of education as they adopted more and more radical changes towards curriculum integration and all age mixed ability grouping has been '...we don't give a damn about PISA. We will do what we think is right for our children regardless of PISA test scores. With just one exception. We do, of course, have to do better than Sweden!!' You need to know a certain amount of Nordic history to see the point of this joke.

The attempt to create a democratic learning community in 1H/2H was a play democracy yet nonetheless real for that. The growth that took place within it was felt by the young people and their parents. These kids really did recover, to a considerable extent at least, from the uncaring willful damage done to them by the politicians, psychologists and bureaucrats who, without a trace of empathy or evidence, wrote off their life chances at the age of eleven. At least that is what the ones I am now in contact with tell me. It is truly shocking that politicians still talk of this time as some kind of golden age of grammar schools while forgetting entirely, or never even beginning to understand the damage being done to the other 85% who did not get into them.

The trust that grew out of the 1H/2H class democratic community visibly and measurably restored their innate love of learning. The freedom to explore their own interests and to share them with others in a secure environment over which they had substantial control turned the learning taps on to full flow. They began to ask their own questions and generate their own purposes. Sometimes alone and sometimes with others. Bruner's three 'C's - curiosity, collaboration and competence - were in top gear (1960 and 1967). The output was phenomenal. The creativity was palpable. There was as much poetry as prose from the kids, some of whom had hardly written anything before. They all learned to speak in meetings and to teach their own discoveries to the rest of the class. The scores in the one standardized test were way above expectations for such a group.

The rebirth of confidence was observed by parents. The maturity that developed was commented upon by teachers who also wanted a new kind of relationship with young people – most notably and significantly those of art and drama. Visitors were impressed by the responsibility that they saw in action. The press was surprisingly kind and constructive on the whole, and both the head teacher in the first year and the acting head in the second were totally supportive. Both had the courage to take a chance on a maverick.

As well as wanting to see a recovery of the will to learn and to develop oracy and literacy I also wanted to help the class members develop the more subtle and hard to teach qualities such as respect for others, how to share and at times take sole responsibility for something on which others depended, to be courageous, to develop a feeling for justice and morality, to be able to trust and be trusted, to be able to participate in a democratic community.

I believed, as I was to argue many years later in the development of the English citizenship curriculum with Bernard Crick (1998) and others, that these qualities could only be learned experientially. A person learns to be moral not by learning about morality from a text-book and getting a good mark in a 'morality' test but by having to participate in daily decision making in a 'just community.' The same applies to democracy, human rights, courage, trust, respect and justice. It also applies to the spirit of social and economic entrepreneurialism. These qualities need to be experienced in real life situations - though they can be mightily reinforced by stories of people who have themselves displayed them, such as Nelson Mandela or Martin Luther King.

At the time I had no knowledge of the work and theorising about stages of moral development of Kohlberg (1987) and Gilligan (1982) which support these what were at the time 'hunches.' I did however have the rich library of stories told by A.S. Neill and Homer Lane in which they give many examples of children recovering the capacity to trust through being trusted, learning to be responsible through being given responsibility, to respect the rights and diversity of others through having their rights respected. It is all so obvious!!

Yet in England now so much teacher energy and student yearning for understanding and respect is being squandered in the damaging, test-ridden, regimented, anxiety driven, school uniform obsessed, competitive, day prisons that we are allowing our schools to become.

Love and kindness are being squeezed out of our schools despite the brave efforts of many teachers.

Chapter 13 – The Importance of Democratic Structures and Human Rights

My vision was that schools should be mini-societies within which students could both learn about democracy and, of equal if not more importance, how to make it work through direct experience. This was in contrast to the conventional authoritarian school where I regarded learning about democracy and human rights as analogous to reading holiday brochures in prison. I was not in a position to do this for the whole school but I could make a start in my own class. By the end of two years the ideas were beginning to permeate the school.

I deliberately tried to enable the students to create systems over which they could take as much control as possible and within which I could be an equal participant as much as possible. My aim was that before very long every student in the class would have the experience of holding some position of responsibility in the belief, with Kohlberg (1987), that responsibility is learned through being responsible for something. This requires freedom to make mistakes. A robot cannot be moral though it could probably get top marks in a morality examination if appropriately programmed.

In fact, over the two years of 1H/2H every member of the class over time held at least three such positions with all having the experience of chairing a meeting. The connection between taking responsibility and becoming responsible quickly became totally self-evident. This was equally true for the understanding of democracy, human rights, morality, justice, and the rule of law where the natural sense of fairness of the students was given conceptual and practical tools for the creation of a just community. The starting point was the democratic class meeting. This was the key contribution that I was able to make. From it, all the other developments emerged.

The class meeting

The democratic learning community of 1H/2H evolved into a clear structure or framework the first key part of which was the class meeting. It is so simple to introduce. It can be practised in any class in any school. I had learned from my work in the therapeutic community, my teaching practice experiments, from Neill's books about Summerhill, and later validated by Kohlberg's descriptions of his Just Community Schools, that the circle provided a shape in which no seat was more important than any other. Popper's case for the capacity of democracy to produce creative innovation more effectively than dictatorship (1945) was amply demonstrated. It was my intention to ensure that everyone would learn how to speak in meetings and that before too long everyone would have the experience of holding a position of responsibility within the community.

Meeting in a circle was a given from our first gathering as a class when I had arranged the seats in a circle before the class arrived. It immediately presented a challenge, both to those who normally sat attentively at the front expecting to be noticed first by the teacher, and to those who attempted to hide at the back and never be noticed. It also gave me the opportunity to step down from the expected place of teacher authority at the front of the class though initially I was perfectly prepared to play that part from within the circle. My power was not just shared with other individuals but with the group of equals while we were in that context.

I wanted the class to use the meeting as a forum not just to express their ideas but also to become courageous speakers who could argue against received wisdom and at times to responsibly challenge power in the form of me as class teacher. To learn how and to dare to speak truth to power. To learn how to be assertive without becoming aggressive. To speak with integrity and not just for effect or to impress. This happened.

I wanted the qualities of democratic leadership to emerge in all the members of the class. The hope was that all would learn the discernment required to judge when they should step forward to lead and when they should leave it to others – and at times to just go their own way alone. This happened in the meetings and the range of learning groups where decisions were made.

At first there was a tendency for a few to press forward and, due to their popularity, be chosen first for key posts. This quite quickly changed as more became willing to be nominated and at the same time the students learned that popularity was not necessarily the best quality for a job to be done well. The skills required for negotiation also developed quite quickly as did the understanding that to get part of what you want is usually better than getting nothing. Sharing, negotiating and collaborating became the norm. Those with the biggest egos gradually learned that they did not automatically have the best solutions. This lesson was learned by the whole class who became discerning as to what qualities, knowledge and skills could provide the most useful leadership in different contexts. The students who organised the meeting for Jo were not the best at organising the class football team who in turn were not the best at organising the lunchtime disco and so on.

I should stress that my vision of the circular class meeting was rather different from the notion of 'circle time' which has emerged some 20 years later through the advocacy of Jenny Mosley (1996) and others. My intention was to share power and not merely provide a vehicle for children to become more articulate and able to formulate and communicate ideas. It was not merely to calm the class down and create a more peaceful and orderly classroom. The democratic meeting was there to make decisions and to see that they were carried out in the same fashion as an adult council or parliament and at the same time it was also a place for all to learn to participate. It was not to be just a talking shop but a place where responsibility would be shared with me for outcomes as well as decisions. In that sense it represented a classic example of a Vygotskyian 'tool as result.' (Holzman and Newman,1993). It was both a tool for the achievement of something else and it was also the 'something else' at the same time. It was to teach democracy while at the same time being democracy.

The class meeting became key to the oracy that rapidly developed in the class – and not just a willingness to speak in front of others but to think about what you wanted to say in order to present an argument that would persuade others. To do this learning to listen was crucial and this skill also developed through discussions in the class meeting in a way that 'hands up' 'me, me, me' in a teacher led discussion rarely achieves.

The idea of democratic decision making through voting was introduced before the end of the first meeting with the realization that an elected chairperson was the best way to decide the order of speakers, to ensure that no-one who wanted to speak was overlooked, and to ensure that speakers stuck to the point in question. At the second meeting the need for an elected secretary to create minutes of the meeting was recognised so there could be no argument about what had been discussed and what had been decided at the previous meeting.

Originally, I wanted to see the role of secretary rotate along with that of chairperson. In reality this did not happen and the same person did the job throughout the two years by popular acclaim because he was so good at it. I was pleased that it was a boy in a role that was widely assumed to be a girl's job at that time. He provided a great role model of civic duty for others. He had much unhappiness in his personal life caused by the death of a younger brother and I think the job gave him a sense of security and stability. This was my view and that of his mother who was a great supporter of the class democracy. Every member of the class did gain experience of chairing meetings however.

There was much discussion throughout the two years of the hazards of decision making by majority vote. We talked a lot about the rights of minorities and they were put into practice by the class in their '5 hands up and 5 minutes quiet' law for example. I told the class early on in our project that Hitler had been elected by a majority vote in 1933 and that one of his first subsequent actions was to abolish democracy in Germany.

I also told them of the practice of consensus that I had seen used in Quaker business meetings later developed into the concept of consent in the sociocracy currently used with imagination and effect in some Dutch and German private democratic schools. Although I knew of the work of Kees Boeke at his innovative Werkplaats in the Netherlands (Simpson, 1954) I did not know of his creation of sociocratic methods of making decisions in communities (Boeke 1945). On balance I still favour majoritarian decision making but I recognize that I have a lot to learn about the sociocratic approach and look forward to visiting some schools where it is practised.

On several occasions members of the class who had lost a vote on some issue proposed that consensus should be used for our class meetings. It was usually opposed on the grounds that nothing would ever get decided. With hindsight I regret that we never tried it. The decision making did become more sophisticated over time and by the time 1H had become 2H it was rare for a final decision on an issue of any importance to be made at the first meeting that it was discussed especially if there had been a narrow vote. The issue would be put on the agenda for the following meeting to give everyone time to think and to lobby others to change their minds. Votes were regularly changed between the first and second meetings however.

Again, with hindsight I regret that more emphasis was not put on human rights education. In our discussions on decision making the rights of minorities were discussed and the right to free speech regularly cropped up in deliberations affecting the class newspaper. I did on a few occasions refer to the United Nations and the Council of Europe and to the importance of human rights. I had copies of the United Nations Universal Declaration of Human Rights from 1948 (United Nations, 1948) and the European Convention of Rights agreed in Rome in 1950 (Council of Europe, 1950) but I made too little use of them.

The project happened well before the emergence of the UN Convention on the Rights of the Child in 1989, nonetheless I could claim with confidence that if one were to time travel to 1H/2H in 1969/71 most of the articles of this Convention would have been seen at work in our day to day practice – in particular article 12 '...the child has the right to express views on all matters affecting him/her...'; article 13 '...the child has the right to freedom of expression, including the right to seek, receive, and impart information and ideas of all kinds'; article 14 'The right of the child to freedom of thought, conscience and religion shall be respected'; article 19 '...the protection of the child from all forms of physical or mental violence...'.

I believe that 1H/2H would have measured up well to the criteria of the current English 'Rights Respecting Schools' programme and done rather better than many schools that have received its accreditation (Hannam, 2011).

The class court

The idea of the rule of law was introduced through the passing of class rules and the creation of the second pillar of the democratic framework, the class court. It represented a major force in the protection of the rights of members of the class as did the second-year committee acting as a court for the entire year group in the second year of the project.

As teacher I always made it clear that 1H/2H existed within the wider frameworks of the law of the land and the rules of the school. That left plenty of scope for class rule making. Again, I made it clear that I was under legal contract of employment to ensure that the class was a safe and orderly place for learning but that I had no wish to involve myself with 'class control' if they could do a better job themselves. I was willing both to share 'authority' and 'power' with the class with the proviso that if their methods did not work then I would have to step in to keep order and to keep my job.

This led to interesting discussions about dictatorship and what would happen if parliament, the police and the courts were to ever lose control of England.

The element of play emerged through the creation of more and more rules, procedures and official posts such as class time keeper and recorders in the offences 'book', many of which seemed doomed to failure to me. I thought that it was important that experiential learning should take place and that I should not intervene unless a procedure appeared to be dangerous. In reality my judgments were sometimes, perhaps often, proved wrong and the student created procedures worked better and with more fairness than anything that I could have created.

Once the rules or class laws began to be created the question of enforcement arose. As Mary Baginsky and I (Baginsky and Hannam, 1999 and Clay,

Gold and Hannam, 2001) and, more particularly Lynn Davies (Davies and Yamashita, 2007), have observed in carrying out research into the functioning of school councils it is not entirely unusual for school students to have some say in the making of certain rules and codes of conduct. It is very unusual, however, for students to have any say in the enforcement of those rules. To me this represents a colossal lost opportunity for learning.

It is a well-known fact that the majority of the UK population are in favour of capital punishment for the crime of murder. It is less well known that whenever there is a free vote in parliament on the issue it is rejected by a large majority of MPs. The reason for this is that they have to bear the responsibility for seeing that such a law is enforced and they know the facts about irreversible wrongful conviction.

In a similar fashion having to take responsible for enforcing laws generates a much higher degree of responsibility amongst the law makers in a class meeting if they might be called upon to serve as magistrates in the class court, or sit on the class jury, or serve as class officers responsible for recording and reporting offences. I later discovered the work of Peter Gray (2013), Danny Greenberg (1992), and Lawrence Kohlberg (1987) all of whom place great emphasis on students carrying out the law-making and judicial roles within democratic schools, as both a tool for good management and decision making, and as a rich opportunity for learning. When I later learned of Kohlberg's ideas of moral development (1987) and the importance of experience and responsibility in its development what happened in 1H/2H made complete sense. The students regularly showed a more subtle grasp of the motivation of offenders that I would have done and also in the creation of the most effective and appropriate sanctions. This is fully supported in the extensive literature describing the functioning of the judicial committee (JC) at the Sudbury Valley School at Framingham, Massachusetts (Greenberg et.al. 1992).).

Bullying hardly ever happened within 1H/2H as the bullied had immediate redress from the class itself with no 'grassing' to teachers being involved. Bullying was regarded with contempt by the class and severely dealt with if it ever arose. The initially shy and less able to defend themselves quickly learned that the 'system' was there for their benefit and, if they had the courage to use it, it would protect them. By the time they were in the second year the class had developed a subtle understanding of the motives of the bully and, when once controlled, how important it was to try to help them. The 'story of Jo' already told in chapter 11 is a typical example of this.

Years later in 2000 when Ofsted (the English school inspectorate) attempted to close Summerhill School, because of its refusal to insist on compulsory attendance at lessons, Suffolk Social Services department in its own much more positive inspection report on the school stressed the child protection aspects of the democratic school meeting (Suffolk County Council, 1999). The report stated that any kind of bullying or child abuse would be virtually impossible in an environment of openness where there was a forum that children were accustomed to use to bring up any issue of concern to them. Mary Baginsky and I in our research into effective school councils, conducted for the NSPCC in 1999, came to similar conclusions (Baginsky and Hannam, 1999).

The class newspaper

This emerged next and was the third prong of the democratic structure after the meeting and the court.

So much written work in school, and especially that set for homework, is of no intrinsic interest to children whatsoever. It is totally irrelevant to their real lives. The class newspaper was an attempt to challenge this conception that most of the class had of 'writing' from their primary school experience. I wanted to see relevance and intrinsic motivation at work. The newspaper quickly came to consist of every available square inch of classroom wall that was not door, window, blackboard or light switch. (In fact, I did not use the blackboard much but the class kept it free for a presentation space for students to use when giving lessons on their projects.)

Anyone could propose to the class meeting that they should edit a newspaper column on any topic that they liked. It was an outstanding success. Over time everyone in the class played a role in this. At times there were rival columns on the same topic, especially sport and music. It provided a magnificent opportunity to insist on well-presented and well written work as public comment provided a critical audience. No-one would try to read an illegible report on the performance of the class football team - or if they did there would be loud complaints. In fact, the sport and music columns produced outspoken argument and disagreement, which I found very satisfying as it was evidence of avid reading.

The physical boundaries between the many columns of the newspaper moved frequently due to incessant demand for space. This caused many disputes and it was decided at the class meeting that an overall editorial committee consisting of two boy and two girl 'column' editors' should be elected. It in turn made decisions such as that any article that had been up for more than two weeks had inevitably become 'boring' and should be taken down by the columnist themselves. If they did not do so the editorial committee would assist by doing it for them. A class law was passed stating that only newspaper column editors could put up new articles to combat the tendency of one or two class anarchists who enjoyed putting up their own articles wherever and whenever they felt like it.

The newspaper was an excellent example of a 'territory' where virtually total control could be taken by the children right from the start with little need to negotiate with me as class teacher. I had my own small space for official class notices which was probably the least interesting of all – and the least read! It also encouraged virtually all members of the class to read and write because they wanted to and not just because I wanted them to 'for their own good.'

I set very little homework beyond a general encouragement to 'write something interesting' for the class newspaper. Two and a half walls of a large classroom always full of material which eventually overflowed onto the pillars between the windows. Nothing was 'up' for more than a day or two except for football league tables before having to give way to new material. This flow never ceased throughout the two years we were together.

I still have much of the material. Detailed accounts of international, national, inter-school and inter-class football and cricket matches often ran to several sides of school writing paper. Reviews of new pop music and children's books were regulars. So much poetry emerged that it had to be collected into booklets which were printed off by the school secretary and sold to parents to raise funds for materials for the newspaper.

Sometimes a short story would appear and more occasionally somebody would write a serial that would appear in parts. One boy regularly wrote rather violent crime stories which occasionally caused me some concern but I resisted the role of censor. There was a regular fashion column to which girls and boys contributed which evolved into regular fashion shows at lunchtime. The cookery column often contributed to practicals in home economics where the subject teacher was supportive of the class democracy and that in turn led to 'tastings' in class.

For a time, there was a series of articles called 'Jobs People Do.' This involved roving reporters arranging to interview people in jobs in school such as the groundsman and the caretaker, but also trips out of school to interview the local police inspector, fire chief, head teachers of primary schools and bank manager. Interviews about the work of parents became a feature. I kept a quiet record of who was writing what for the newspaper in my official 'mark book' which led me on occasion to encourage a relatively non-contributing student to produce something on a topic that I knew to be of particular interest to them. This led to several 'break-throughs' of enthusiastic productivity. The key was relevance and intrinsic motivation. My 'encouragement' represented no more than an injection of a bit of self-belief that they could do it.

One boy who lived on a small holding struggled with punctuation and spelling. He believed that he could not write and that little of his knowledge was of any value. I asked him what kind of article would he like to read in the class newspaper.

His reply was 'something about tractors, but nobody writes about that.'

'Who could write about that?' I asked.

He thought for a bit and laughed – 'I could. You are tricking me into writing something Derry.'

'Exactly,' I said. 'How do you know that there might not be many people interested in tractors and you are the only person who could do it.'

He asked me to help him with the spelling. I said 'yes, that's part of my job as teacher – but you can check the technical stuff from your dad's farming magazines.'

This discussion took place on a Friday. The following Monday he appeared with twelve pages of fairly misspelt and totally unpunctuated writing but with every technical word absolutely correct such as 'king-pin' or 'power take off'. We spent a lunch hour getting the first two pages into publishable form having negotiated with the Hobbies Editor for space in her column. The desire to have the spelling and punctuation perfect came not from me but from the author. For the first time in his life he wanted his writing to be read by others. This perfectly exemplifies my desire for the newspaper to became a place for writing that was relevant to the children's interests and generated by intrinsic motivation. Paul's next project was a 'Guide to dealing with difficult births when lambing.'

Chapter 14 – Non-coercive Relationships and the Importance of Play

No less important than the structure of democracy as an organising idea for the democratic learning community were the relationships that I hoped would emerge.

I wanted to see coercion and the need for it to fade away even though coming to school was legally compulsory. I disliked the individualistic and competitive relationships that existed between the students and the fear-based relations between teachers and students in my grammar school. They seemed to me to produce what Winnicott describes as 'false selves' where the deadness of boredom and disinterest prevailed (1964, 1973). I wanted to create 'holding environments' that were psychologically 'safe spaces' fit for Winnicottian 'true selves' to freely develop the life, spontaneity, creativity, motivation to learn and empathy for others that I believed nearly all young people possessed, or could learn, with perhaps the exception of the severely genetically autistic. I thought that that kind of environment could support a few disturbed children who had experienced the lack of what Winnicott describes as 'good enough' parenting which might cause them to behave in anti-social ways. The class meeting, rules and court that later broadened into the whole second-year did indeed develop the strength to protect these 'holding environments' from such anti-social threats of a minority of disturbed children.

I believed with Bruner (1960, 1967) that young human beings are by nature curious and collaborative and I sought a convivial environment in which collaboration and mutual respect between the students would be the norm together with the opportunity to develop his third 'C' - competence. I was also attempting to create a teacher-student relationship that was not based on fear of authority or fear of failure, backed by coercive threat of punishment. Instead, I sought an ethos grounded in mutual respect between human beings of different ages. I expected no automatic respect as teacher but sought to win respect by being respectful and by exercising the minimum amount of authority necessary to allow the democratic structures.to emerge and grow in strength.

On the other hand, I hoped to ensure that the class felt, if only tacitly, that I could if necessary, impose order just as any other teacher would if the community created self-managed 'holding environment' temporarily could not cope with a disruptive threat. At the same time, I tended to allow more disorder to emerge than most teachers would have tolerated believing that this would provide problems that the class could then learn to solve.

In a way I was playing at not being fully in control even though in order to survive, especially in the early days, I never allowed the kind of chaos that would attract the adverse attention of the head teacher. I was quite explicit with the class about what I was doing. I explained that I could keep 'teacher' discipline if I had to but would much prefer to share and, if possible, hand control over to them for at least some of the time that we were together. I also made it clear that I could and would take power back again if necessary. It could be argued that this created an 'unreal' situation and I would agree to a certain extent. In my view I was creating a 'safe' space within which 'power' could be 'played' with. Sometimes the students knew that they were acting 'as if' they had real power but that they would be protected from being harmed or causing harm to others if things got out of hand. For most of the time they 'played at' or 'imagined' they were in charge 'as if' they really were in charge and I believe learned to handle power and authority as a result. That was my intention and that is certainly what the alumni that I have spoken to 50 years later remember. In my experience young people of this age still have no problem in dealing with the 'as if' quality of play though school all too often attempts to snuff it out.

The question of forms of address arose when the class began to go on field trips organised initially by me, and later by the class itself. Once out of school it seemed natural for the students to address me as 'Derry' just as they were addressed as 'Andrew' or 'Shirley' by me. At first, I made it clear that I had to become 'Mr Hannam' again once back at school as this was the requirement of the school rules – or so I believed. I later discovered that in fact there was no school rule on the subject, merely a convention, so I ceased to correct anyone calling me 'Derry' in class. I explained that it might cause me problems if they did it in front of other teachers and this was respected almost totally apart from the odd slip.

As a junior teacher I felt that I would be giving an unnecessary hostage to fortune in pushing the issue too hard though I never understood why the English teaching profession requires such formalities. Respect is not won in this way as anyone who reflects for a minute on their own secondary school experience will realise. The issue arose again in every school that I have worked in. As my position in the school system became more senior over the years, I became personally more relaxed about relating to students on mutual first name terms remembering Geoff Cooksey's keys to a good school - 'Christian names and Carpets Derry!'

This issue has always caused some discomfort in some colleagues who equated formality with respect. Perhaps it is cowardice on my part that although I have never insisted on anything other than mutual respect between adults and young people, I have never insisted that all staff use their first name with students. Once a critical mass of teachers and other adults shift to mutual first names it just becomes harder and even pointless for the others to hold out for formality. With hindsight I now feel that this position was a bit of a 'cop-out' or evasion if we were genuinely trying to move towards a more democratic position where power and responsibility were shared. Several members of the second-year humanities team gradually adopted my policy on first names but others did not.

We now know enough about brain function to be more or less certain of what I then only suspected, namely that fear and learning are incompatible. Fear kicks-in the 'fight or flight' mechanism in human beings and when this happens the learning centres in the brain shut down. Why politicians with their obsession to introduce more aggressive discipline and testing into schools do not seem to know this is beyond my understanding. I think it is because there is no tradition of pedagogy as an academic discipline based on research in the UK. Everyone thinks they know all that there is to be known about how to make children learn. It is common sense and obvious they believe. The resentment and underlying feelings of injustice that such a regime induces are conveniently forgotten. As adults they would bitterly object to being treated in such a fashion yet for some reason it is acceptable to subject children to such regimes.

In reality the result is to create an environment that is not conducive to learning. It leads to 'resentful going through the motions' in some and 'even more resentful switched-off disinterest' in others though short-term retention of superficial knowledge for regurgitation in tests may be achieved. The resort to 'more discipline' is failing in many schools. It says 'we know it hasn't worked so far so let's have more of it.' It is rearranging the deck chairs on the Titanic. It is producing neither more order nor more learning in many cases and even when it appears to work it is usually merely modeling the worst of hierarchical power and its abuse.

It is for sure no way to develop an understanding of democracy, citizenship and human rights. We need less fear and anxiety and more intrinsic motivation and stimulation of interest in our schools for deep learning with understanding to become the norm for all students. There is so much to be learned in this respect from the relaxed but stimulating environments of the best early years education such as that of the Reggio Emilia programme in Italy (Cadwell, 1997).

Certainly, by the end of the first term relations between class members and between the class and myself had become relaxed and totally respectful. Bullying within the class had virtually disappeared and I have no recollection of needing to reprimand anyone with any degree of severity. There is no mention of any such event in my extensive contemporaneous notes. Together we had created a near perfect environment for learning. This is also the recollection of the class alumni with whom I am in contact. They remember the atmosphere as friendly and safe and one in which projects could be pursued without interruption or disturbance from others. Coercion had effectively disappeared as I had hoped that it would.

Chapter 15 – Curriculum, Streaming and Selection, Oracy and Literacy, Assessment and Learning

Curriculum

In my experience of being at school and in teacher training I saw little interest on the part of the school in the interests, hobbies and prior experiences of the students. Yet my primary school teaching practices had shown me what a powerfully motivating source of learning these represented if taken seriously as a significant part of the curriculum. Though I was under some constraint to adhere to prescribed curriculum content from the heads of subject departments I was determined to open up as much time as possible for the students of 1H/2H to pursue their own interests. My key input in both contexts was to encourage students to ask questions at all times. This fitted well with the way in which the class meeting and class court functioned which was around the constant questioning of proposals and of the explanations of behaviour offered by defendants in the court.

At times this took on a Freirian tone of critical pedagogy (Freire, 1970; Shor, 1996). I encouraged the discussion of questions such as 'why is there an 11+ examination?' 'Why do fifteen per cent of students in our town go to grammar schools whereas thirty per cent do in Wales?' 'Who decides what we should have to learn in school?' 'Why do we have to wear school uniform when my friends in Germany do not?' Also, more existential questions such as 'Why are we here?' 'What is the meaning of life?' 'What is love and does it matter?' 'What happens when we die?'

As more and more students chose to work on projects related to the local town questions such as 'why do some people live in big houses and some in very small ones?' 'Why are there homeless people on the streets?' 'Why are there private schools?' 'Why are there very rich people and very poor people?' tended to arise naturally. And be the source of endless debate.

Gradually more and more time was opened up to student interest project work until in the second year it constituted perhaps 50% of humanities lesson time, or 30% of total curriculum time. If the time allocated to the class meeting and the class court was added to this the prescribed curriculum was being squeezed into about 25-30% of allocated time in my class with something similar happening in most of the other six classes in the year.

Almost no time was allocated to the topics initially prescribed by the subject heads as the humanities team much preferred to create its own subject content with specialists within the team preparing material and sharing it with other team members. Students were encouraged to work with others interested in the same content but individuals were perfectly free to go their own way if they were alone in their interest.

The role of the teacher in this situation became that of facilitator helping students find appropriate material and information and above all encouraging students to ask questions of their information rather than just regurgitate and copy material from encyclopedias. This was of course long before the days of the internet and Wikipedia! The results were as surprising as they were pleasing. Once students were studying topics in which they were intrinsically interested the idea that there were 'lazy' or 'easily distracted' or 'inattentive' students simply ceased to arise.

These are all perfectly rational responses to being forced to learn 'stuff' that has no interest or meaning for the learner. I found that because a lot of freedom was provided for pursuing individual or group interests there was a general willingness to put up with some class teaching from me. Initially I suggested and encouraged the presentation of finished projects to the rest of the class and/or as contributions to the class newspaper but after a while it just became a collective assumption that this would happen. Generally, the class was very supportive and forgiving if a presentation was not wildly interesting as the agreed and expected time was 5-10 minutes.

The curriculum thus became substantially negotiated and student driven. The variety of topics was vast over the period of a year. Sometimes parents became involved and came into class to work with a small group or to talk to the whole class about their interests and occupations. Gradually teachers began to give talks to other humanities classes. Eventually the second-year team was allocated the school hall as a learning area in addition to its seven classrooms. Teachers from the team, and eventually other teachers who happened to be free, would give talks either on topics requested by the students or on their own interests and hobbies. Students could attend if they wished whether the content was pertinent to their own current project or not.

They often went to a 'lecture' just because the topic caught their imagination or perhaps because they just felt like a break from their project. This was recreating the open lecture system that I had enjoyed so much in my year at Oxford University. One of the most popular was a slide show presented by a science teacher on the 'History of the Railways in our town.' About 60 students attended and enjoyed it so much that the teacher was pressed to repeat it. The students learned a lot and the teacher was delighted that his hobby was so interesting to young people. I was delighted to see the students learning that enthusiasm for learning should never stop in human beings however old they were.

Theoretically of course there is nothing surprising in all this. The idea of building on existing knowledge and scaffolding new learning within a 'zone of proximal development' has been introduced from Vygotsky to current educational thought via Jerome Bruner and Lois Holzman (1997). It was entirely possible, when learning in groups, for students in the 1H/2H context to facilitate new learning for each other as well as this being an important role for the teacher. What strikes me as strange and even absurd about the current interest in the ideas of Vygotsky is that I often hear it said that the job of the teacher is to undertake this role while class teaching. It is nonsense to think that 30 individuals can be drawn into identical 'zones of proximal development' at the same time. Each individual will inevitably be in a different place. That is the whole idea!

Streaming and Selection

Attendance at these voluntary lectures involved students from all kinds of backgrounds and past academic performance apart from the fifteen per cent who had been selected out for attendance at the local grammar school. The absurdity of this 'once and for all' selection process became very obvious as the previously unrecognized enthusiasms of students began to blossom. In my two primary school teaching practices there had been no selection by past performance or 'academic ability', either by 'streaming' for individual subjects or 'banding' for groups of subjects. Students learned with those with whom they shared interests whatever their so-called 'prior attainment.' The environments had been totally non-judgmental, which was how I wanted it for 1H/2H.

In my secondary school teaching-practice there was academic streaming for every subject and the results were very much in line with the research evidence. There was little of the movement between streams that should have been expected as different students developed at different rates. The 'top' streams were allocated the 'best' teachers and were largely middle class. The 'bottom' streams were largely working class, were allocated the 'weaker' teachers, and inevitably became difficult to manage once they realized they were the 'rejects.' Little learning took place in these classes.

I have since read a great deal of research evidence on the subject of selection by ability. The findings are mixed, but there are certainly strong indicators that learning is just as good in mixed groups as in selective groups for the more 'able' students, and very much more effective for the 'average' and 'less able' students so long as appropriate teaching methods and teaching materials are used. The damage to self-confidence and self-esteem caused by selection is of course entirely removed.

These findings support the view that good teachers are required for mixed 'ability' classes. But surely all students are entitled to good teachers at all times? It is no surprise to me that the national school system that regularly tops the league table PISA/OECD (OECD, 2009) charts for effective learning in mathematics, science and mother tongue is that of Finland (Sahlberg, 2013). Where, incidentally, the charging of fees for education is substantially illegal reducing the private sector to a handful of international and religious schools funded by the state. Regular delegations are sent from the English ministry of education and Ofsted to report back on how it is done (Ofsted, 2003). They rarely seem to notice that any kind of streaming or banding by academic ability has been expressly forbidden in the Finnish Peruskoulu (nine-year comprehensive school for 7-16-year-olds) since 1985, or that all teachers in Finland have to have studied to master's degree level.

As a result, research is finding that in contrast to what is to be observed in most developed nations, there is a growing disconnect between parental wealth and educational outcomes in Finland (Pekkarrinen, et.al. 2006). It is quite outrageous that English politicians vie with each other to be seen to be the 'toughest' on streaming without any understanding of the research evidence whatsoever. At the time of writing the English school inspectorate (OFSTED) is forbidden to evaluate a school as being 'outstanding' unless it subjects its students to 'streaming.' As a one-time accredited Ofsted inspector I feel ashamed to be associated with an organization that can operate on such a non-scientific basis.

Even in mathematics, where the case for streaming is most commonly accepted without question, the work of Jo Boaler shows that deeper understanding in the subject is best developed in mixed ability classes (Boaler, 1997 and 2013). As an inspector I came to expect to see teacher-controlled streaming at work in most mathematics lessons in most secondary schools.

One interesting exception was a large rural school in the Midlands where students placed themselves into the maths 'stream' where they felt most comfortable. Despite the anxieties of the mathematics inspector students rarely seemed to make inappropriate choices, there was much more movement between sets than in most streamed contexts, and the examination results at GCSE were significantly higher than would have been expected in a school in that kind of socio-economic environment. The students made more appropriate decisions than the staff, and the teachers in that school had the wisdom to recognize this.

Fortunately, there was no selection at work in any subject that affected 1H/2H and none developed in any of the classes of the first or second-year humanities teams, unless it was the result of student self-selection around a particular interest.

Oracy and Literacy

Perhaps at this point I should refer to the predominant issue for which I was centrally responsible as the 1H/2H humanities teacher was oracy/literacy. This, together with numeracy and an understanding of science, are the three curriculum areas on which international comparative studies are usually focused (OECD 2009) and over which the English state school system is attacked for failing large numbers of English young people. In 1H and 2H we almost entirely ignored the prescribed exercises and compulsory homework provided by the English department. Oracy and literacy improved with virtually no compulsory or coerced activities at all.

Oracy developed naturally through the class meetings, the class courts and the project presentations. If challenged I planned to defend the amount of time allocated to the democratic processes as opportunities to speak clearly and thoughtfully in front of others. In fact, the need for such a defence never arose. Both parents and the head teacher saw the point entirely and observed the results in the children. The tendency for project work to be presented to the whole class similarly added to oral skills.

The phenomenal amount of poetry written by virtually all the students and read to the class was a bonus as was the willingness of many students to read passages from the 'class story.' The class story I should explain was a book recommended by a student or a group of students for reading to the whole class by me and willing volunteer readers.

I quietly and privately used a reading test that I had found in my last practice primary school. It purported to give an approximate reading age which I shared with students if they asked. Again, this was partly because of my own inexperience and partly as a defensive measure. I inherited no non-readers at the start of 1H but there were quite a few 'reluctant' readers who had learned that they were 'slow' or 'behind' at primary school. By the end of 2H all the students were either at or ahead of their chronological ages according to this reading test and at least half just read straight off the end of the test which stopped at 13 years 9 months!

Reading of the class newspaper was incessant. We had a growing number of willing readers of fiction in the class whose recommendations were voted on at the class meeting. I was surprised at just how popular this was. The book review section of the class newspaper was read by most. The class meeting voted for a 'story time' or a silent 'reading time' of ten minutes at the end of every humanities session. I did not insist that reading done in 'reading time' should be of fiction though mostly it was with 'good books' being passed from student to student. At times the class tax fund was used to buy several copies of a popular paper back as the humanities teachers had virtually no budget – books were supposed to 'trickle down' from subject departments and on the whole did not do so.

It was not until the second term of the second year that the acting head teacher agreed to remove a proportion of the budget from the subject departments and allocate the funds directly to the 'lower school humanities' programme. The various subject heads thus kept control of providing or funding the logistics of an approach that several of the most powerful, such as the head of English, fundamentally disagreed with and disapproved of! This caused some ridiculous problems such as separate exercise books being allocated for each subject even though most of the work was either integrated or project based.

All the students wrote for the class newspaper at some time or another and some wrote continuously. There were reports and articles on every subject under the sun, book reviews, short stories often with endless episodes, and many, many poems. Although own choice projects could be presented in any form with drawing and photography being used sometimes, writing was the most common medium. There was a great incentive for accuracy and legibility as so much of the writing was for public consumption. It was designed to communicate and not to be 'marked' by the teacher.

Some students wrote plays for the drama club and others wrote narrations for fashion shows. There was no resistance to written 'work' as is so often found in students of this age – and other ages! I would often teach mini-lessons on commonly occurring errors and would, usually at the individual's request, sit with those who struggled with spelling, punctuation, or other aspects of grammar. Students asked each other for help and willingly gave it as a matter of course. The accuracy of the written English in the presentations and in the newspaper was consistently high and commented upon by visitors. The half dozen class dictionaries became well worn. All this was pre-digital and I can only imagine what a difference the internet would have made to the presentations and the volume of writing.

Although there was scope for creative expression through stories, plays and poems there was little scope for the visual arts in the humanities area of the curriculum. Despite this, presentations occasionally involved graphics of one form or another, illustration and sometimes photography.

Plays were written for the class and later for the second-year drama club, but drama was taught as a separate subject on the timetable. However, the drama teacher was a great supporter of the humanities project and would often use students' humanities stories, plays and poetry as stimuli for his work.

The truly expressive medium that became amazingly popular in humanities sessions was poetry. This started in 1H from the very earliest lessons where I introduced the three-line discipline of the haiku. After only one lesson students were writing them at home. One particular boy who had almost totally refused to write at his primary school started writing dozens of haikus. His parents were spellbound and came to school especially to tell me about it. His father, an academic scientist at a local university, told me of his own struggles with writing. He believed it was the combination of precise meaning and precise structure within a tiny three-line format so that so appealed to his son.

I raided the English stock cupboard and the school library and my own home library for poetry of all kinds. The students also brought books from home from Wordsworth to Spike Milligan. We began to produce printed anthologies every half-term which were sold around the school and to parents, the proceeds going into the class fund.

One of the most exciting creative outcomes was the way in which the art teacher used the poems as stimulus for visual art. Art was also a separately taught subject and the art teacher was also a great supporter of the humanities project and in particular for the 1H/2H democratic learning community. On several occasions we had poetry readings in the art room against a backdrop of student painting and drawing. Students would be allowed, or even encouraged, to make art work for their humanities projects in art lessons.

Learning and Assessment

There were no tests for the whole class, though one student had seen a 'spelling bee' on television in the United States and persuaded the class meeting that it would be fun to have regular spelling bees in class, with a prize for the winner. I was not wildly enthusiastic about this as I did not want those who struggled with spelling to feel exposed. I proposed that entry to the 'bee' should be voluntary and this was agreed. In reality almost everyone took part. Usually I set the words to be included but not always. In fact, I think a lot of learning resulted from this as it was fun and free from 'failure anxiety.' It was not compulsory and only a handful of students would cope with the very complex words of the final. Nobody seemed to mind that it was always the same three or four students who made it to the final as nobody was forced to feel stupid in front of the others.

The accommodation provided for the second-year humanities team was a collection of classrooms on two corridors. Although humanities was timetabled for all the classes at the same time the team never achieved the creation of interest groups of students from different classes to any significant extent, although individuals could go to another teacher's room for specialist help so long as that classroom door was open. If the door was closed it meant that the teacher was teaching their class and not available to visitors from other classes. (Cross-class working groups happened as a matter of course in my next school where we had a purpose-built part open plan humanities department.)

However, there was a steady flow of students moving between classrooms most of the time as they learned which teacher had the best specialist knowledge on particular topics. This created a challenge to the school norm of one teacher in one classroom with unaccompanied student movement in lesson times being firmly discouraged. As long as it was happening just within the humanities corridor the acting head raised no objections, though there was a certain amount of staffroom muttering by teachers from other departments.

The evidence for what was being learned came partly from displays, written work in writing books, and folders but most impressively from the presentations given by students to the rest of the class. Nothing reinforces learning more effectively than teaching it to others. We would agree deadlines for presentations to the class but in 1H/2H these were never strictly adhered to as students could never be sure in what directions a project would lead or what new material might turn up.

The presentations tended to happen as and when they were ready to happen.

Occasionally there would be a protest that everyone had to stop what they were doing to listen to a presentation that they were not very interested in, but generally the class spirit was such that everyone showed interest in what everyone else had been doing. Not least because they would expect similar interest to be shown for their presentation!

I was always available to help and made sure that students were asking their own questions to give their projects 'edge' and purpose. It was suggested several times in the class meeting that attendance at presentations should be voluntary and that they should take place in the school hall that we had use of for most of the time. This was always voted down by the meeting as the majority view was that the class should show interest in each other's carefully produced work and that people would feel hurt if nobody came to their presentation.

Unfortunately, presentations by students to other classes as a whole, or to interest groups from all classes, did not happen, though the idea was beginning to be discussed in humanities staff meetings and by the second-year committee towards the end of our time together.

I monitored the work in progress fairly inconspicuously and graded the presentations in semi-secrecy only giving my opinion when it was sought. I never 'marked' anything produced by students in the conventional sense of writing on it in red or any other colour ink. I would sometimes send them notes keeping copies myself pointing out errors especially if they had asked me to do this. I encouraged the use of dictionaries and made sure that there were always at least six in the classroom. Some students bought their own. Significantly they were often borrowed and not returned for some time.

Generally, there was a strong desire to get anything in writing well presented with correct punctuation and spelling as others were probably going to read it. I participated fully in the questioning of presentations and sometime this would go on for much longer than the agreed ten minutes.

Sometimes students would take the questions on board and add additional pieces to their projects. The quality of these discussions was high and sometimes took on form of investigations now to be found in the work of Philosophy for Children (P4C) described in the work of Matthew Lipman (2003) or Patricia Hannam and Eugenio Echeverria (2009). The idea of students becoming the teacher at this time and the teacher becoming the learner seemed to be an effective motivator for all – including me. So much was learned about such a range of topics that I was not at all surprised that 1H scored so highly on the Bristol Achievement Test when it was administered in the third term of the first year.

At one point in 2H so many members of the class were involved in some sort of study of the local town, anticipating the ideas of Fielding and Bragg (2003) about 'students as researchers,' that it effectively became a 'whole class' project involving a wide range of investigative field trips, interviews, and speakers coming into class. This was how I first developed ideas about Community Education and Community Schools later conceptualised by writers such as John Sharp (1973), for whom I was later to work as his head of humanities. Sharp, with Cyril Poster (1982), Stewart Mason and Andrew Fairbairn in Leicestershire, all built upon the ground-breaking work of Henry Morris in the Cambridgeshire villages colleges (Ree, 1971).

These field trips using the town as a resource for learning eventually developed into field trips, for half the class at a time, to the New Forest and then to Wales. The students worked in groups to study aspects of the areas that interested them in advance and planned visits to places that hopefully would be of interest to all. Using tents in the New Forest and out of season holiday accommodation in Wales all would be responsible for some aspect of cooking, washing, and keeping the building or tents tidy. The students insisted on having 'field-trip class meetings' while we were away from the school to manage these arrangements.

Things often went hilariously wrong, like 60 bars of chocolate melting into the sleeping bags, or live caterpillars crawling out of the salad. My wife would bring our four children in our safari Land-Rover with cooking utensils and supplies and I would bring 16 students at a time in the school minibus. These were wonderful trips, remembered vividly by the class alumni that I am currently in contact with, and led to vast quantities of displays and presentations from coal mining to ponies, border castles to royal hunting privileges.

The largely student driven curriculum with much opportunity for collaborative learning totally convinced me of the correctness of Bruner's three Cs - curiousity, collaboration, and competence - when given the opportunity to blossom (1960, 1966). Similarly, the ideas of moral development through experiential learning in managing a democratic community developed by Kohlberg were visibly working in the rapid development of care for each other and for the class community as a whole. Moral learning was happening through the incessant requirement to resolve moral 'dilemmas.'

I constructed sociograms every half-term without explaining what I was up to. I asked every student to name the two students they would most like to work with on the pretext that I might need to construct some learning groups for teacher led lessons and this would help me to make sure that everyone was put into a group with at least one of their choices. My real purpose was to monitor the popularity of some students and the tendency to isolation of others.

Over the two years of 1H/2H there was a steady tendency for popularity to become more diffuse and isolation to diminish. I think this is extremely significant and demonstrates the growth mutual respect and tolerance of diversity that grew within the class. Exactly what I hoped for and, I believe, evidence of Kohlberg's ideas in action (1987). Knowing what we now know about the sheer scale of bullying, disturbed behaviour, fear of failure and mental health issues in our schools this was quite an achievement and a major vindication of the project.

In the early days there might have been a slightly unhealthy side to this in that the 1H kids showed some signs of thinking of themselves as an elite and better that the other classes in the year. However, I am sure this diminished over time and certainly there was little sign of it in the second year of the project when they had the opportunity to share their ideas with the other classes.

This level of student participation in curriculum decision making led to what I have come to describe as a benign cycle of learning though I am not totally certain of the correct order of factors -

CHOICE – OWNERSHIP – INTEREST – ENGAGEMENT – SELF EVALUATION – RESILIENCE – SUCCESS – SELF ESTEEM – MOTIVATION – DEEP LEARNING – UNDERSTANDING.

It seems to me to be possible for all schools to create come curriculum space for this student driven learning to take place. Yaacov Hecht, a friend and colleague from the international democratic education movement, and I have launched a '20% campaign.' Our idea is that one day a week in all state schools everywhere should be dedicated to curriculum that is generated from the interests of the students and negotiated democratically with the staff. The proposal was very well received at the 2016 Council of Europe World Forum for Democracy through Education by a plenary session of over 1000 participants.

Chapter 16 — Education for Citizenship, Human Rights, Sustainability, Entrepreneurship

The 1H/2H project took place long before the need for citizenship education was being discussed widely either in the UK or in Europe as a whole. 'Civics' education existed but from my limited experience seemed to be used as a time filler for older so-called low ability students who regarded it as boring and useless. There is now considerable international evidence to support this impression (Torney-Purta, 1999). The 1H/2H project was clearly an experiment in education for democratic citizenship as were my further attempts to develop school democracy in more senior posts in other schools.

These provided the inspiration for my later work with the Council of Europe Education for Democratic Citizenship project/Human Rights Education (EDC/HRE) which adopted a requirement for student participation in decision making right from its inception in 1997 (Council of Europe, 1997). A year later when Bernard Crick became adviser for citizenship education to David Blunkett (education minister of the new labour government) I was able to work with others to inject similar thinking into the English Citizenship Curriculum that emerged in 2000 from the 1998 Crick Report (1998).

It was possible to support the argument that student participation in decision making leads to enhanced learning in a pilot study that I was commissioned to carry out. This became known in citizenship education circles as the 'Hannam Report' (Hannam 2001, Potter 2002). The findings supported the idea that schools that made serious efforts to involve as many students as possible in democratic processes actually achieved better academic results than other schools in similar social environments, together with better attendance figures and fewer exclusions for anti-social behaviour. The legal requirement for all students in secondary schools to experience 'participation in democratic decision making and responsible action' introduced in England in 2002 was removed in 2010.

The many ways in which some English schools were able to involve students in decision making processes between 2002 and 2010 are listed here though not all would usually be found in any one school –

- through formal structures of student participation – class, year, house, school councils in the school (Clay, Gold and Hannam, 2001)
- representation on town, county, national/international school student organisations – e.g. COPS (Council of Portsmouth School Students)/ Student Voice/OBESSU (Organising Bureau of European School Students' Organisations)
- student involvement in school governance (Hallgarten, Breslin and Hannam, 2004, and Hannam 2005)
- student participation in curriculum decision making with senior teachers and department committees
- joint student/teacher led programmes of 'electives'
- students as researchers (Fielding and Bragg, 2003)
- peer mentoring, teaching, counselling
- students involved in appointing staff
- student enterprises
- student led community service projects – changemakers
- student evaluation of teaching
- student led courses for new teachers
- student led eco/environment groups
- student radio, tv, newspapers
- Philosophy for Children – p4c (Hannam and Echevarria, 2009)
- Rights Respecting Schools (Hannam, 2011)

It is somewhat ironic that employer's organisations which generally support right-wing governments are complaining at the time of writing of the poor communication skills possessed by many school leavers in England. These are the very skills developed to a high degree within the 1H/2H project and which are developed through the participative activities generated by an imaginative citizenship curriculum. In fact, in all my work to develop student participation the emergence of entrepreneurial skills has been evident, with communication being a central factor.

The skills required for making a social enterprise such as a drama club, or a not-for-profit enterprise such as a shop to raise funds for a charity, or a for profit business that fills a demand such as selling refreshments and snacks at break times, are very much the same. The ability to spot an unfilled need and to organise the means to fill it are identical as is the imagination, energy and willpower required to make something new happen. I did not need to encourage this process – it just happened in an unstoppable fashion once the appropriately supporting, encouraging and nurturing environment had been created.

In 1H/2H clubs were forming all the time many of which spread into the whole second-year. At times there were rivalries between individual class clubs and second-year clubs. There were games clubs, drama clubs, pop music clubs, dance clubs, fashion clubs, football and cricket inter-class leagues, debating clubs, chess clubs, field-trip planning groups, a bird-watching club, a model railway club, a stamp collectors club. Virtually all these clubs involved a degree of fund-raising. Sometimes the fund-raising was club specific and would involve a 'pay-to-enter' lunchtime fashion show or disco. IH/2H also created its own taxation system to fund projects that everyone in the class would benefit from. The class meeting passed a law with a unanimous vote in its first-term that everyone should pay one penny per week to the elected treasurers for the purchase of games for the games club and for a padlock with which to secure the games cupboard.

It was agreed that, as I had more money than the students, I should pay sixpence a week to the fund. I also kept a supply of pennies in my desk drawer which I would give or lend to anyone who for whatever reason could not afford to pay their weekly tax. It was never more than about ten pence but nothing was ever stolen in two years.

The management of the clubs, like the class newspaper, were areas where students could be totally in control and free to make and learn from their mistakes, and where adult supervision was substantially not required. The class meeting provided the forum for coordination if club requirements for the classroom were not compatible. However, it would not be accurate to describe these activities as 'extra-curricular.' In my mind they were entirely part of the total learning experience offered by the democratic learning community and as such firmly part of the curriculum.

In recent years the Brazilian entrepreneur Ricardo Semler (1988) has shown dissatisfaction with the failure of the Brazilian school system to equip young people with the creative, innovative, entrepreneurial and communicative skills that he looks for in his employees. He has discussed with an Australian psychologist friend of mine what kind of school could do the job. The specification is not very different to 1H/2H. In similar fashion Ken Robinson has had millions of hits for his Ted Talks on YouTube lamenting the tendency of school systems all over the world to actually cripple and destroy the very creativity in children that our twenty-first century economies are crying out for.

Greed, grotesque and accelerating inequalities of wealth (Piketty, 2014; Wilkinson and Pickett, 2010), contempt for democratic politics and politicians, xenophobia, fundamentalisms of many kinds, fueled by the violence of the excluded, are gaining ground. Rampant, under-regulated, sustainability disregarding, dysfunctional, capitalism and communism are in danger of wrecking the ecosystem of our planet. Imagination and creativity of the highest order will be required of our young people if they are to have any chance of reversing current trends. These qualities were very evident in 1H/2H 50 years ago! Visitors regularly commented upon the capacity of the students to ask questions, to persist in seeking answers, to think critically and creatively, to take initiative and to accept responsibility.

Why are such educational experiences still so rare, and possibly becoming rarer, today? Can anything be done?

CONCLUSION – Can State Schools today move towards becoming Democratic Learning Communities?

I often talk with many young teachers in the UK who feel that my story is now a pipe dream. They believe that curriculum and teaching are now so totally circumscribed by prescription, absurd levels of high-stakes testing and mechanical tick-box inspection, that the freedom that teachers once possessed in the days of 1H/2H are long gone. They experience anxiety levels in the face of testing, classroom observation by school managers/leaders, and inspection that I could not have even begun to imagine in 1969-1971. This is demonstrably the current reality in too many of our schools and I cannot argue with them beyond checking that my retired union membership is up-to-date.

Many, and often the best, leave the teaching profession within a year or two of joining it and fewer are being recruited year on year. What I say in response to their feelings of despairing exhaustion and urge to find another career is 'you can always do something – it is the system that is wrong, not you and certainly not the kids! It is always possible to share some decision making with your students, though this is easy to say and hard to do.'

The opportunities and space for freedom and creativity for teachers has to be made by those responsible for school leadership. They must develop a vision that moves on from the nineteenth century 'factory/industrial' model that we are still stuck with. They have got to be prepared to show some of the courage of the head teacher and the deputy head teacher that I worked for with 1H/2H.

There are things that they can do.

They can simplify the timetable to allow teachers to work in less fragmented periods of time.

They can allow teachers to work in teams again despite the subject rigidities of the national curriculum, so that teachers in the arts or the sciences or the humanities can work together to integrate their prescribed curricula in innovative and collegiate ways.

To do this effectively they need time to talk and plan as was provided in my beginning years as a humanities teacher and is now provided within working hours in Finland. This may well mean a shorter school day for students. Again, this presents no threat to standards in Finland so why should it in England. Plans to extend the English school day deserve the question, 'if what you are doing is not working then is more of the same likely to bring improvement?'

I have argued above that there is no valid scientific case for separating students into 'ability' groups and that countries that refuse to do this have more successful schools.

Equally, if we accept the evidence that different students develop their understanding at different rates at different times there can be no valid arguments for teaching groups narrowly defined by age. It is perfectly possible to create a structure where students of different ages who share similar passions and enthusiasm can work together. I have seen this happening in small primary schools and the handful of English state secondary schools that have all-age 'elective' programmes.

To bring about the kind of community identity that 1H/2H developed, and that later extended to the whole second-year, identifiable physical territory needs to be provided for which the students can be held substantially responsible. This can then be used by them to create a rich structure of curriculum supporting activity over which they have substantial control.

They can make time available for meeting. As I have said, time must be available for planning and reflecting meetings for teachers and democratic meetings for students. Class meetings, year or house or school council meetings need to be allocated sufficient time within the normal teaching day to do their job effectively. Assemblies can then become at times just what the word implies in its political sense – opportunities for larger groups to meet at which representative bodies can explain their thinking and listen to comments from the floor. where Votes can be taken that involve whole sub-school communities and not just representative minorities. Such assemblies happened on a regular basis between the second year and the second-year committee and were always totally orderly events despite the participation of 230 young people.

It is important that school leaders become entirely opportunistic in their approach to involving students in decision making processes.

In 2001 I was involved in lobbying the then junior education minister, Cathy

Ashton, to include students as 'stakeholders' worthy of representation on English school governing bodies. This became permissive law in the 2002 Education Act which enabled governing bodies of any state school to appoint students as non-voting 'associate-governors'. The English think tank 'ippr' created the 'I Was a Teenage Governor' project in 2004 which monitored the progress of governing bodies that chose to incorporate students as 'associate-governors.' The findings were entirely positive (Hallgarten, Breslin and Hannam 2004; Hannam 2005) yet many state schools still do not even know that this legal possibility exists.

School leaders should encourage students to get involved in student organizations covering more than one school such as the city-wide COPS (Council of Portsmouth School Students). This grew out of a programme created jointly by Michael Fielding, then of the University of Sussex, and the City of Portsmouth Education Department from 2002 to 2006. The city was struggling with low academic standards and chose to develop Student Voice as one strand of development for their improvement. All eleven secondary schools and thirty plus primary schools together with special schools and pupil referral units (PRUs) took part. I had the privilege to work with David Hart, the city citizenship adviser, on the Student Voice work. School councils were created where they did not already exist in all of the secondary schools and many of the primary schools. These were encouraged to work in clusters with special emphasis on the primary/secondary interface. After three years preparatory work representatives from all the secondary schools and special schools were invited to a meeting in the City Guildhall to launch a city-wide school students council in 2005. It decided at its first meeting, which I chaired for just the first 15 minutes before supervising the election and handing over to a student, to call itself COPS.

It still exists fifteen years later. After ten years COPS had negotiated a number of citywide improvements for school students enabling and encouraging groups to visit each other's schools. This despite the fragmentation of the city's school system into academies and multi-academy trusts. It is to the credit of the headteachers that despite this fragmentation they have all continued to support COPS.

After ten years it evolved into a not-for-profit business called UNLOC which, while maintaining its COPS function with the city's schools, now goes way beyond the city limits to help young people to start their own businesses across the South of England. It employs ten people and uses a suite of offices in a neighbouring Further Education college where it is actively supported by the principal as well as members of parliament from all parties.

In 2018 it held a well-attended reception at the House of Commons. One very appropriate outcome is that the one-time local authority adviser, David Hart, on his retirement has become an employee of UNLOC developing their work in Africa and answerable to a board chaired by a one-time student representative on COPS.

Having regularly taken groups of English school students to international gatherings organized by the Council of Europe in conjunction with the very effective OBESSU (Organising Bureau of European School Student Unions) based in Brussels. I have lobbied for years for the creation of an English national school students' organisation. After a false start in 2005 with ESSA (English School Students Association) a more securely grounded Student Voice was set up by students in 2012 assisted by the Phoenix Education Trust which will hopefully eventually become a member of OBESSU. In some countries, most effectively perhaps in the Nordic nations, school student organisations are taken very seriously by government education ministries.

In Norway and Denmark for example the school students' organizations are automatically consulted by the Education ministry together with parents and teachers' bodies before any organizational or curriculum change is enacted.

In Norway the school students initiated 'Operasjon Dagswerk' where every student goes to work for one day. The wages earned are collected nationally and a substantial sum of millions of NOK (Norwegian crowns) is awarded to a 'charity or cause of the year' selected democratically by the students. Also in Norway, the school students' organization has successfully lobbied parliament for more effective anti-bullying legislation that can lead to the imprisonment of a negligent head teacher who takes no effective action after incidents have been brought to her/his attention. At least six members of the Norwegian parliament, the Storting, have been board members of the school student's organization (EON). The Norwegian prime minister said to me at a meeting in Strasbourg in 2016 that '...I cut my political teeth in EON board meetings.'

The good examples of highly participative state schools that already exist in England need to be better known as models for other school leaders. There are not that many but they do exist. Schools such as the Ian Mikardo High School, or School 21 in London, the XP School in Doncaster, or Wroxham School in Potter's Bar come to mind. The entire network of Cooperative Schools is also moving firmly in the direction of collaboration rather than competition and this needs to be more widely understood.

There needs to be a better understanding amongst school leaders of international trends, networks and examples of democratic schools where there is freedom to learn in innovative ways. These include the nationally funded democratic schools network in Israel with its research and training base in the Institute of Democratic Education – a body that has full accreditation powers for awarding degrees and diplomas for teachers.

The Nuestra Escuela network in Puerto Rico is impressive in creating democratic learning communities for young people rescued from the gang culture that scars or destroys many lives.

In the United States the network of schools modeled on the pioneering Sudbury Valley School in Framingham, Massachusetts is now speading statewide and worldwide with 'Sudbury' schools in many countries.

There is an international democratic education conference (IDEC) that rotates around the continents of the world that is little known in England though it has existed since 1993. When it met in Devon in 2011 it was well attended by teachers and students from the two English independent democratic schools, Sands School and Summerhill School, but virtually no teachers attended from the state sector even though state school teachers from places such as the United States, Puerto Rico, Taiwan, Japan, Australia and South Korea travelled long distances to the event. When the conference met in Berlin in 2005 and Leipzig in 2008 large numbers of state teachers and academics from the universities in which the conferences were held, attended.

Similarly, in 2012 when the conference was held in Puerto Rico many state-school head teachers, education academics from several universities, government education administrators, the leaders of the island's teacher unions and the governor's personal adviser for education, together with the leaders of alternative programmes, all met and reached system changing understandings.

There are now continental organizations networking democratic and innovative schools such as EUDEC (European Democratic Education conference), APDEC for the Pacific area, INDEC for the Indian sub-continent. EUDEC conferences were recently held in Greece (Crete 2018) and Ukraine (Kiev 2019) which were attended by many state school teachers from those countries. If the Corona virus allows 2020 will see the EUDEC conference arrive in Bulgaria.

The Council of Europe launched its Education for Democratic Citizenship/Human Rights Education (EDC/HRE) project in 1999 with student participation in democratic decision making as one of its key 'pillars.' It has run many courses for teachers over the past 20 years with an emphasis on programmes in Eastern Europe. It funds two well-resourced centres – one in Strasbourg and the other in Budapest where I have had the privilege of facilitating courses not just for teachers but also for students in conjunction with OBESSU.

In 2017 the government of Norway created the 'Wergeland Centre' in Oslo which works closely with Council of Europe in Strasbourg. It has run programmes of Summer Academies to develop democratic practice and understanding in a number of Eastern European countries. There is immense potential for synergy and collaboration between its work and that of EUDEC. In 2018 the small democratic school in Berlin, Netzwerk Schule, attended a conference on school democracy in Oslo along with many state schools from all over Europe.

Almost weekly I discover more and more schools, existing or starting up, or just in planning, that are trying to find new ways to foster learning in contexts that refuse to judge, grade and divide young people from each other. That build on all that we know about the importance of networking, play, self-directed learning and creativity. That create a context of accepting relationships of equality and respect between adults and young people. That use the issues that always arise when people live and work together as opportunities to learn in communities based on free speech and democratic decision making using some form of school meeting. That challenge the coercive systems built around anxiety, fear of failure and competition.

On the day that I am writing the closing words of this book I discovered a fast growing network of such schools in Poland and at the same time learned of a beautiful school in Galicia, Spain called Escuela O Pelouro where children with various conditions that are normally diagnosed as 'problems requiring special education' learn naturally and freely alongside those who do not experience these difficulties. In my inbox is another story of a democratic school in Portugal called the Escola Da Ponte, the ex-principal of which, Jose Fransisco Pacheco, has now moved to Brazil and is building democratic community and educational networks in Sao Paulo.

Models for the future exist now in growing numbers. Over thirty such schools have opened in France, fifteen in the Netherlands, five in England, one in Wales, and four in Ireland in the last few years. We all need to learn from them. I hope that my small experiment in one class and later in one year-group in a South Midlands secondary modern school between 1969 and 1971 provides a modest but significant pointer and contribution towards this future. It was set in and represented a small step in the rich, though all too often neglected, traditions of English progressive education. I often felt alone but I was not. Others were independently struggling to realise the same vision, also struggling to create spaces in which young people could be free to learn about the world and create a new one in their own ways.

The usually small, private, and fee-paying democratic schools should be seen as 'pioneers of possibility.' They provide examples of what can be achieved when teachers and young people are freed from the burden of prescribed curriculum, imposed high-stakes testing, single-age cohorts, behaviour management policies, fear of failure, isolation and exclusion. They demonstrate what can be achieved when students are freed to learn in self-directed ways, set in contexts that recognize their full human rights in schools that are self-governing democratic learning communities.

My final word will come from the mouth of a well-known Californian educator who heads the highly successful media-arts programme at Palo Alto High School and who advocates for 20% of curriculum time to be immediately put into the hands of students – something she has practised for thirty-five years. She is Esther Wojcicki, mother of the CEO of YouTube Susan Wojcicki who herself is a product of a similar 20% policy of self-directed time operated by Google. It is encouraging that Esther was invited to co-author the recent report on the future of teacher training from the influential Economist Intelligence Unit, "Staff of 2030: Future Ready Teaching" (2020).

Esther's keyword is TRICK (2019). T for Trust; R for Respect; I for Independence; C for Collaboration; K for Kindness.

The story of 1H/2H is not finished and the need for its 'message' is anything but over.

The last word from Esther Wojcicki - **TRICK**.

***

AFTERWORD – WHAT DOES IT ALL MEAN FOR THE FUTURE AND THE FOURTH INDUSTRIAL REVOLUTION?

"WE HOLD THE KEYS TO THE FUTURE – AND SHOULD NOT BE AFRAID TO SAY SO!!"

(A revision of Derry Hannam's keynote talks at the EUDEC conferences held at Korfes, Crete, in August 2018 and Kiev, Ukraine in August 2019)

I am going to talk about what is wrong with most of our schools and school systems – and then what democratic education can contribute to improving things so that we can face the challenges presented by the fourth industrial revolution (4IR). I will refer to my own experiences as a teacher and inspector in England.

What's wrong with what we have now? Well I think that the English philosopher Bertrand Russell and the American philosopher John Dewey were correct when they said that authoritarian schools offer young people the choice of becoming either submissive or rebellious – and that neither provides a good preparation for living in a democracy or taking responsibility for their own lives. That is still the case.

The same idea is expressed in the 2016 policy document of the Ukraine ministry of education entitled "The New Ukraine School." (Part of a major programme of reform in a remarkably progressive direction in Ukraine since 2016.) It lists the qualities required by young people today and tomorrow, all of which I agree with – creativity, critical thinking, goal-setting, teamwork, communication. It powerfully describes the failure of your existing school system to generate these skills.

It states that most Ukrainian schools just stuff kids' heads with more and more out of date information and then test their memorisation of it. Thereby generating maximum anxiety, mental ill-health and damaged well-being, none of which is conducive to deep and meaningful learning. This sounds familiar - just like England!! The Ukrainian document creates an unforgettable metaphor in describing a typical Ukrainian school student as being "...like a stuffed fish. It looks like a fish but it cannot swim!!" I guess that we are here today because we agree with this point of view – to some extent anyway.

To reinforce the point, I will repeat a few words from the brilliant piece that won the Scottish Schools Young Writer of the Year Award in 2018. Written by a 16-year-old, Harriet Sweatman, it speaks for millions of British and probably Ukrainian young people who are trapped in our anxiety ridden, testing obsessed, PISA performance driven schools that more and more come to resemble day prisons.

She writes:

'...We are told that if we are not fit to work, then we are worthless. There is no love in learning any more... we envy the people who have left school already... Whatever happened to expanding your horizons? Assignments where you can research what you want count for nothing... Finding out who I am and what I care about is unimportant. I have been flattened by a concrete curriculum so structured and unforgiving that I have forgotten how to function without it. With no bell throbbing at even intervals and no grading to build our lives around how will we cope?... They say that high school is the best years of your life – but not in this world, where qualifications matter more than personal qualities. I feel that I have grown backwards, as if I know less about myself and who or what I could be than when I started... The curriculum must release its chokehold on the throats of this nations' children and let them breathe...But for us it is too late. For now, we just have to wait until the final bell rings and we walk out of the school door for ever.'

Twenty years ago, at a Council of Europe conference on how to teach democracy and human rights, I said that 'learning about democracy and human rights when I was at school was like reading holiday brochures in prison' and that 'you can't learn to swim if you are not allowed in the water!' Democracy and respect for human rights require skills as well as understanding, they have to be practised in the everyday life of the school and not just talked about by teachers. According to Harriet nothing has changed.

The 'other way' that I found both necessary and possible as a teacher could be described as 'democratic education.'

What do I mean by Democratic Education? I mean two things. Two pillars or principles on which Democratic Education is constructed.

The first I call SPDM – 'student participation in decision making' – where young people choose what and how they will learn. Where learning is self-directed and self-managed, free from coercion, competition, compulsory testing (though not if self-chosen) and fear of failure and where, above all, young people learn to manage their own time. I would like to bring an end to meaningless schoolwork that is preparation for meaningless work. Much meaningless paid work in the wider world is coming to an end anyway, which I am totally in favour of so long as we have democratic control of the consequences! We in the democratic education movement aim to create schools where children can think and choose for themselves. We no longer want to produce obedient clerks, factory workers and soldiers.

The second pillar I call SPDDM – 'student participation in democratic decision making' – where young people and staff decide together how the class and school communities will be managed; democratically and with respect for human rights. These school communities of learning and decision making should not be too large. Maybe 150/200 maximum. The number that can attend a school meeting and know who everyone else is. In my experience large schools need to be broken down into mixed-age 'schools within schools' of this size. These, in turn, should be made up of home groups of perhaps 30 maximum, again of mixed ages where it is possible for everybody to speak and be heard.

Both these pillars or principles are needed for young people to discover their own purposes and to be able to create their own identity. This is already important and will become more so as the Fourth Industrial Revolution unfolds. Its artificial intelligence, robotics, machine learning all threaten the capacity of 'work', or rather, full-time paid employment, to provide security of identity for most of us as much of this paid employment will cease to exist.

Only a few per cent of people will be required or know how to create and develop the high-tech world that is advancing like a tsunami. The rest of us, supported by some form of universal basic income, currently being trialled with success in places such as Canada and Finland, will need to be able to create our own identities for ourselves. It could provide us with time to enrich our own lives and the quality of our democracies.

Schooling as we know it does not help young people prepare for this. We need another kind of school where young people can discover and develop in freedom their own talents, purposes, and passions and, at the same time, learn to manage democratic societies which respect human rights. Coercive authoritarian schools do not and cannot do this.

Then there are two parts to our task.

First, we need to continue to develop and support fully democratic schools and learning centres that are "Pioneers of Possibility". Places like Summerhill School in England and Sudbury Valley School in the United States that go a long way fast. They provide us with working models of what can be done. They will often be small and privately owned. Though this will not always be the case as in Denmark, for example, it is still possible for a group of parents to get state funding for a democratic school. Israel is now providing state funding for democratic schools such as Hadera School, pioneered by Yaacov Hecht, who spoke to us earlier in this conference.

There are whispers that a little-known government fund in the Netherlands that exists to fund otherwise unfundable projects might soon be paying for the strong network of Dutch democratic schools that currently charge fees.

These pioneers of possibility need to stay within the laws of our nation states, even though at times this can be difficult and we may have to defend ourselves from the law on occasion. We have had some success in this regard, such as the famous Summerhill case in England where an aggressive inspectorate was defeated in court. In the Netherlands the initial hostility of the Dutch inspectorate to the Sudbury model democratic schools led to the closure of De Kampanje School. But, after much struggle and negotiation, the school has been resurrected in the form of the new school at Harderwijk, which is now used to train those self-same inspectors! Sadly, there is a darker side to this picture, such as the closure of the highly successful Ammersee Sudbury School in Germany now confirmed by the Bavarian court.

I love the story told by the Bulgarian group at this conference where the Bulgarian minister of education is reported to have said that "...everything that you propose is illegal – but do it anyway." Funny but not without risk!

The second part of our task is more daunting.

It is crucially important and easy to neglect when we come together to enjoy each other's company. We must never give up the struggle to change our state public school systems. Here we will probably not be able to bring about great change overnight but will need to work incrementally in achievable smaller steps. Not giving up when two steps forward seem to be followed by one and a half steps back. Why? Because it is where most of the kids are!

Some European state school systems are already more student-centred, more equitable and more amenable to democratic change than others. Finland, where the school students themselves have created a 'Demokrati i Skolan' project jointly with the education ministry, and the other Nordic countries may be the most potentially democratic. Even Sweden, which is currently recovering from its socially regressive neo-liberal school system experiment, is producing a literature supportive of more school democracy. More typically the school system in my country England (we have four different education systems in the UK) and in Greece are probably amongst those most resistant to change.

"The New Ukraine School" document refers to schools needing to become places that no longer reproduce the poverty ladder, but instead leverage social equity, consolidate communities of creative and responsible citizens who are active and enterprising. This is all great – BUT – why there is no mention of democracy – or human rights. I am puzzled by these omissions and hope to discuss them with you later in the conference.

The task of creating the necessary change is not easy. It will be a struggle to change the 'stuffed fish' schools. It will cause anxieties for teachers and uncertainties for parents and students. We have to be supreme opportunists!! How we do it will depend on how we can adapt the two key principles of curriculum choice and democratic learning communities to the realities in which we find ourselves.

Some school students are already demanding changes to the school curriculum. Not all young people are as depressed as Harriet Sweatman. OBESSU (the organising bureau of European school student unions) has been arguing for change for 40 years. They have been waiting for a uniting issue such as the overwhelming imperative of resisting climate change. I am very excited by the 'Greta Thunberg phenomenon' where demand for school change is indeed being driven by the students themselves led by the courageous sixteen year old from Sweden and now spread to 36 countries at least. I am sure that you have all heard of her school climate strike movement. I joined 1500 young people in my home town of Brighton a few weeks ago. Many of the young strikers that I spoke to knew more about climate change than their teachers, parents or political leaders. schools to become centres for 'sustainability action.'

A group of highly articulate and well-informed young people in England have created the "Teach the Future" campaign that is lobbying parliament for complete curriculum revision around the issue of climate change. They want to see schools become centres for 'sustainability action." 200 academic experts in the field have backed the students in the press as well as members of parliament from across the political spectrum.

In Germany Angela Merkel has contradicted German Education Officials to support the student strikers as has Leo Varadkar in Ireland! In the UK the government and most head teachers threatened the students with punishment. That will not stop many more young people participating each week in hundreds of towns and cities worldwide.

In England the high stakes testing industry has 'occupied' our school system and we have an exponential increase in mental health problems and self-harm incidents among school students that justifies the use of the term epidemic. The figures increase when the schools are open and decrease during the holidays.

We are about to commence the testing of four-year-olds if the government can find a testing company corrupt enough to do it. The evidence of ALL early-years research shows this to be predictively useless as far as future school success is concerned while it is certainly damaging to the self-confidence and well-being of the children.

So, we have nursery schools dividing children into 'fast tables', 'average tables', and 'slow tables.' That, of course, will have a perverse and unintended predictive effect on the future of those children, especially those sat at the 'slow table.' Meanwhile creativity and the arts are being driven out of the state curriculum by the STEM (Science, Technology and Mathematics) subjects. The good news is that there is a growing resistance from some parents at what they see being done to their children.

Maybe I could mention here the "20% Campaign" which Yaacov Hecht from Israel and I launched at the Council of Europe's World Forum for Democracy through Education in Strasbourg in 2016. The idea is simply that all state schools everywhere should allocate twenty per cent of curriculum time, or one day per week, to be negotiated around the interests and enthusiasms of the students, and perhaps also the staff. Nearly all the 1200 delegates at the Forum voted for the idea and some of those who did not said it was because "...twenty percent is not enough!"

Although I developed the 20% idea from my own teaching experience and from observing 'electives' programmes in some schools when I was an inspector I have since discovered Google's policy of allowing staff to spend this amount of paid time on projects of their own choosing which has led directly to innovations such as 'Adsense' and 'G-mail.'

I recently wrote an article for Democracy Day in England in which I argued that young people needed time to think, time to find themselves and discover their passions, and that currently most state schools do not allow this. In fact, they even follow the students home with more and more homework. The "20% Campaign" represents a 'Universal Basic Income of Time' for school students if you will! – and of course the 20% is just a start.

I am pleased to note that the Economist Intelligence Unit (2020) is now supporting the idea in its latest report on the future of teaching, 'Staff of 2030: Future Ready Teaching.'

It sounds like a perfectly reasonable idea as after all it leaves the state still controlling the other 80% of curriculum time, yet its implications can be revolutionary as it changes the relationship between staff and students from an authoritarian to a negotiated one.

We have to devise as many such 'reasonable' demands as we can and be prepared to argue our case in the national educational press. We need to push to gain access to policy makers. This can be done and I will give an example later in this talk.

School change is also being driven by parents in many countries – for example the first Sudbury School in England, on whose board I am proud to sit, with four similar schools in the pipeline. There are many such democratic schools across Europe and the World. Thirty-five new schools in France alone and fifteen in the Netherlands. Perhaps a thousand democratic schools world-wide?

My own story is one of opportunism, communication and learning to find friends, in order to create change at the teacher level – first as a class teacher, then a senior teacher and later as a school vice-principal.

Why did I bother to look for another way?

To improve learning, to open minds, to think for yourself, to develop curiosity and collaboration, to respect diversity, to see through the violent snake oil of demagogues and xenophobes encouraging us to look for scapegoats for social and economic difficulties.

My ideas were grounded in a long tradition of progressive child-centred education in England, though this is substantially ignored in our current teacher education. It is encouraging to find some of these ideas in "The New Ukraine School." The idea that curriculum and learning should be a partnership between pupils, teachers and parents. That teachers and pupils should relate as friends without fear – and logically that means reducing coercion. Straight from the AS Neill Summerhill song-book!

Of special importance perhaps –

- Recognition of the Human Rights of young people as people, now and not just as future citizens, though I began my work before the UN Convention on the Rights of the Child existed.

- Jerome Bruner's three 'C's describing the nature of the young human animal – Curiosity, Collaboration, Competence.

- And my own belief supported by psychologists such as Lawrence Kohlberg and, more recently, Peter Gray in his work on the importance of play (2013), that many important things can only be learned experientially; such as morality, responsibility, Human Rights, democracy, justice and the Rule of

Law, social and economic entrepreneurialism, human relationships that are based on trust and mutual respect. Most important of all perhaps, how to find and follow your own deepest interests and passions in order to create your own identity rather than being dependent on others for it.

My own experience of school was like that described by Yaacov Hecht in his talk earlier at this conference. "Why are you only interested in what I can't do but not in what I can do and in what interests me?" Unlike Yaacov, I could pass their tests but I found them unbearably tedious and pointless.

My first experience of a democratic institution was a therapeutic community in a psychiatric hospital in the 1960's in Oxford. The treatment was living together in a democratic community rather than pharmaceutical, electrical or surgical. I have no time to go into detail but it worked.

If it can work in a psychiatric hospital then why not a school I thought. So, I decided to train to be a teacher. This was not so simple and as a student I had many arguments with my instructors, not least in psychology which was all behaviourism and behaviour management.

"I want to work with children not Skinner's pedal-pushing rats or Pavlov's salivating dogs," I said. In exchange for not questioning lecturers I was permitted to use the library for private study where I discovered a gold mine of unread dust covered books by John Dewey, Tolstoy, Montessori, Pestalozzi, Bertrand Russell, Homer Lane and most wonderfully A.S. Neill. Time to follow my own interests was the key. Once during my teacher-training I drove past Summerhill School by chance but was afraid to enter the 'Holy Shrine.' That is no longer the case!

I am writing a book about these formative experiences and my first rather extraordinary years as a 'democratic teacher' in a state school that was willing to tolerate, even encourage, innovation.

I managed to do crazy democratic 'Summerhillian' things on my teaching practices as a student. Two, in primary schools, were highly successful and one, in a secondary school, was a catastrophe. I was nearly thrown out for 'allowing' the school students to talk about their feelings towards school in a 'history of democracy' class. The irony went unnoticed by the school!

As a young teacher I had a truly wonderful first job. I was able to create a democratic class with 35 kids who had just failed the high-stakes 11+ test which decided whether 10% or so would be selected for university entrance geared grammar schools. Instead of being fired, as I half expected, the support from parents who saw the self-confidence of their children recover was so great that I was put in charge of all seven classes in the grade – 230 kids – in the following year. We controlled 60% of the curriculum as traditional English, history, geography, social studies and religious education were rolled up into 'integrated humanities.'

It was really possible to use both pillars of democratic education. Students studied what interested them in a context of democratic process. I am still in touch with some of the 'kids' from that first class – now 60 years old and coming up to retirement – and some have contributed their memories to the book. Some define the democratic experience as 'life defining' even though it was only for two years from the ages of eleven to thirteen.

Not everything went smoothly of course. As a new young teacher, I was not very good at explaining my democratic methods to more traditional teachers.

Sometimes I was amazed by the moral sense that developed in these young people when given some power and responsibility to run their own affairs. There was a deeply moving event when a troubled Roma girl, let's call her Jo, was put into my class. She befriended some older also troubled girls and they began to bully and steal from other children – though usually not from anyone in our class which had a class court that they knew would not be afraid to oppose them. A point came when she was about to be excluded from the school. Without my prior knowledge our class met after school one day to decide what could be done to help her. They decided to elect her to be both class chairperson and a class magistrate. She was moved to tears and never stole again.

In retrospect it was great fun and the kids learned a lot. Several eventually went to university, although this was theoretically very unlikely for '11+ failures.'

After two years in that school I was head hunted to be Head of Department in a newly built school of 2000 students nearby. It was possible to introduce democratic methods on a wider scale. For example, students would take over parts of the curriculum in examination classes which they would research and teach to the rest of the class. Each student was given part of the library budget which they could spend alone, or combine with others to buy a more expensive book or books. This being 1973 there was little knowledge of or interest in computers but one boy, Nick, ordered two computer books which he read over and over again. A few years ago he appeared on my doorstep as a man in his late forties – now CEO and owner of a large and highly successful software company in Bristol.

In my third school I was at first in charge of a democratic 'House' of 180 young people aged 11-18. We set up a house council and a house court. We reorganised the house building. House assemblies were democratic affairs where major decisions were made directed by the house council. The house teachers were tutors of groups of mixed ages who, to some extent, chose their own tutor. Wherever possible these teachers taught different subjects to house classes with an emphasis on choice of topic and democratic class management.

Later I became vice-principal and, for a while, acting-principal of this school. The principal and I, with the help of older students and some committed staff, began to change it into a Community School

School and community became 'turned on' to themselves and each other through democratic structures and processes growing out from the school.

It began as a bet between myself as vice-principal and some older students. It was a rural school serving a country town supporting stone quarries and sheep farms. Many students found the town boring and said there were only about 20 clubs and societies with few open to young people. I bet them that there at least twice as many. They conducted a survey. They found over 100 organisations!! The governors (school board), students' council and the parents' association invited them all to a massive conference in the school to explore how the clubs and societies could be more available to young people and how the resources of the school could be more available to the clubs and societies in return.

The results were amazing and led to many new organisations such as a community newspaper, (now on-line and edition 126 just published), run jointly by students and adults and a community orchestra with all ages playing together. Both these organisations still exist forty years later. All the activity was and still is managed and coordinated by a Community Education Council which was often chaired by a school student. We went on to help create an English Community Education Association to create change at national level.

With adults in some classes it became absurd for the young people to have to wear school uniform – so, as a community, we abolished it. This was in 1978. Three years ago I revisited the school and found that with the full support of the parents and the town there was still no school uniform. It remains the only secondary school in this part of England to have no school uniform.

I then became a school inspector. Possibly a mistake as I came to dislike much of what I saw and much of what I had to do. Occasionally I was able to support and encourage head teachers who were trying to fight the waves of centralised curriculum and testing that were beginning to corrupt the system. On other occasions I supported individual class teachers who were trying to be child-centred or democratic in a small way.

When I found a school that was allocating 10% of time to student led elective activities, I was able to say 'well-done' rather than 'you're fired.' And then after 250 inspections I discovered why I had become an inspector.

The government tried to close Summerhill School in 1999 – one of only two fully democratic schools in the UK. The principal, Zoe Readhead, daughter of A.S. Neill, and by now a good friend asked me if I could work for the school against the hostile inspectorate. I did and we won the ensuing court case – though I must emphasise not just because of me!! Many, many people came to the aid of the iconic school and, as well as advising the legal team somewhat secretly, I was also proud to be part of a high-powered and very effective 'alternative inspection team' put together by another friend, Ian Cunningham from the Colleg for Self-Managed Learning in Brighton. I am no longer afraid to go into the 'Holy Shrine' when I drive past as I had been thirty years before!

I would now like to come back to a story that is an example of how sometimes it is possible to change policy at local and national level if we are sufficiently opportunistic.

First, a local example. 15 years ago, with a team from the University of Sussex, we supported or, if necessary, created student councils in all the secondary schools and some of the primary schools of Portsmouth, a deprived city in the affluent South of England with a record of poor and declining academic performance. Representatives from these councils met together city-wide and formed COPS – the City of Portsmouth Students. This has now evolved into a not for profit company called UNLOC which employs 10 young people and provides training in student participation across the South of England. A colleague who was a senior local education officer at the time and who co-ordinated the first COPS meeting 16 years ago is today in Rwanda spreading the work of UNLOC in Africa!

Now an example of change at national level. In the 1990s and early 2000s I had been working on numerous Council of Europe conferences and projects to introduce ideas for democratic pedagogy to teachers, often from the ex-communist countries, and often with the help of teachers from the Nordic countries. I was involved in the launch of the EDC/HRE (Education for Democratic Citizenship/Human Rights Education project). I was also running courses on school democracy for OBESSU (Organising Bureau of European School Student Unions) and involved in research into the curriculum reforms in Norway known as Reform 94 and Reform 97 which introduced more democratic processes into primary and secondary schools. In addition, I was advising the Swedish speaking school students in Finland who in their planning of the 'Demokrati I Skolan' project.

This was the moment of the electoral success of the Labour Party in the UK which led to the Blair government. The new minister of education was David Blunkett who knew that England was one of the few countries in the world not to have a citizenship curriculum. He turned to his old university teacher Bernard Crick to be his adviser and by a series of coincidences I became one of Crick's semi-official advisers because of my growing European experience.

I brought one simple idea to the role. 'If teachers just talk to students about democracy it goes in one ear and out of the other. It has to be practised in the everyday life of the school to be of any value. Otherwise it is like reading holiday brochures in prison.' Crick 'bought' the idea from me and Blunkett 'bought' it from him.

When the law introducing the new curriculum was created it included a requirement that all students in state funded English secondary schools should have the opportunity to 'participate in democratic decision making and in responsible action.' When the chief inspector heard of this, the same one who attacked Summerhill, he claimed in the right-wing press that this requirement would reduce the time for mathematics and other 'serious' learning and thus would reduce 'academic standards.' The minister wobbled and I was asked if I had any evidence that schools that were already quite democratic had results that were at least as good as those that were not at all democratic. I only had anecdotes so I was given a fairly large sum of money and told to see what I could find – by yesterday!!

I found 20 schools in all kinds of socio-economic environments that were significantly 'more democratic than most' and compared their examination results, attendance figures and exclusion rates with the average for all other English state secondary schools in similar environments. In every case the results for the 'more than usually democratic schools' were better than the average. This became known as the 'Hannam Report' (2001) and is available online in several languages. The minister was able to say to his critics 'I have some evidence that you are wrong – do you have any to support your view?' They didn't and the democratic participation requirement passed into law – until it was removed in 2010 by an incoming conservative-led government.

However, during that ten years thousands of English secondary students had an experience of democratic decision making and action that they might not otherwise have had. For me it was worth the effort. Additionally, the Report has made it into the final 30 'studies of merit' (of 3200 reviewed) of student participation research published by the University of Innsbruck meta-review carried out by Nowak and Mager in 2012. Google tells me that it has been cited in 100 or more other studies before and since – so – not a complete waste of time even though I am not a professional researcher but just an enthusiast with a modest M.Phil.

The Democratic Citizenship Education experiment in England has led to other research, mainly in state schools, that supports our convictions though we need much more of it! Overall, I think it can be said that grabbing an opportunity led to meaningful policy change even though It has not survived a change of government. Nothing lasts for ever!

Later I had the opportunity to persuade another minister to change the law to enable students to sit as members of governing bodies (school boards) – unfortunately only as non-voting associate-members. Research showed that schools who implement the opportunity had improved governance as a result of listening to the students.

It is very pleasing to see our democratic education movement beginning to build its own research base such as the doctoral work of Charlie Moreno and Freya Aquarone, both participants at this conference.

But now I come to my main point in this talk.

There is a growing awareness that the nineteenth century industrial/factory model of education is not good enough to cope with the floods of change that are already washing around us. Finland, Canada, Singapore and a few others are already doing something about it, but more widely creativity, innovation, smart communication and digital skills are not being developed or even valued in our schools. In fact, unusual talent is sometimes being labelled and medicalised as attention deficit disorder or ADHD or other 'on the autistic spectrum' conditions. They are given medication such as the soon to be ubiquitous Ritalin and only 14% of those diagnosed ever gain employment. At the same time the UK electronic spy agency GCHQ has released figures showing that 120 of its most brilliant cyber defence employees have had precisely these labels when they were at school but, by good luck and serendipity, have found their way to an employer that understands and values them.

The most common response of UK politicians is "OK the current 150-year-old industrial model of education is not working – so – let's have more of it!! Let's re-arrange the deckchairs on the Titanic!!" But the ship is sinking.

The CEO of IBM said in a recent panel discussion at the World Economic Forum at Davos "It is a waste of time setting young people tests that could easily be answered by computers – they should be learning to do things that computers can't do."

So, we come to the Fourth Industrial Revolution and what democratic education has to say to it.

The First Industrial Revolution was based on steam and iron. It created the first industrial cities at the turn of the 18th and 19th centuries. It led to rapid changes in production and distribution through railways and shipping together with a vast increase in capitalist wealth. The Second Industrial Revolution came at the end of the 19th century with electricity, oil and steel replacing coal, steam and iron leading to the internal combustion engine and powered flight. The third brought the power of digitalisation in the second half of the 20th century. I have heard Alan Turing's breaking of the Enigma Code described as the key event leading to personal computers and the internet, the effects of which are still dominating our lives.

But we are facing a veritable tsunami of change as the Fourth Industrial Revolution reveals its emerging power. Klaus Schwab, the creator of the World Economic Forum, only invented the term in 2016 yet Google already shows more than 40 million results and counting for a search, and there is a very large and rapidly growing literature.

Some of you, mainly under 30 probably, will know and understand more than me about Blockchain and its rivalry with Holochain, Crypto-currency Wallets and Bitcoin (how many of you have one or can tell me who Satoshi Nakamoto is? That is a trick question!!), Machine Learning, Robotics, Nanotechnology, The Internet of Things, Artificial Intelligence and Technological Singularity (the day that robots become more intelligent than the collective intelligence of human beings – maybe 2035 or sooner?), 3D Printing, Autonomous Vehicles or Drone Delivery, and the Turing Test.

Schwab says these new and potentially highly disruptive technologies could enormously expand the numbers of people connected to the worldwide web and that this in turn could massively improve the efficiency of business, of production and distribution. He believes they could even regenerate the natural environment through better use of resources. But – he says less about the increase in the accumulation of wealth by the already super-rich and the potential impoverishment of millions as paid labour declines or disappears. I have seen many figures for this and some optimistic economic historians argue that every industrial revolution leads to the loss of some redundant jobs but that this is always counterbalanced by the creation of new ones.

Most serious students of what is beginning to happen now however predict that the Fourth Industrial Revolution will be disruptive on a wholly new scale. They talk of anything between 18% unemployment (OECD) to 54% (latest Oxford study) with 33% of men between the ages of 25-54 being out of full-time paid employment by 2030. The impact of the Corona virus pandemic is speeding up this process. The Hi-tech industries, the silicon valleys of the world, will need only 1-2% of us to be highly skilled innovators to maintain and develop the new systems and even they are more interested in creative aptitude than qualifications and examination scores. The rest of us will probably need no more than GCSEs or high school diplomas.

Uber has already ordered thousands of driverless cars. Deliveroo riders will soon be replaced by drones. Paid labour is declining as digitalisation, automation and robotics proliferate. Careers are no longer lifelong. Wages have been falling for many together with growing job insecurity in the 'gig economy.' At the same time inequality of wealth is rapidly increasing as we see the rapid exponential rise of the 'precariat.' (Those whose paid work is without benefits such as paid holidays, sick pay, pension rights and is in every way precarious.) Their jobs will be the first to go – and they vote for Trump or Brexit.

We know from the work of epidemiologists such as Wilkinson and Pickett (2010, 2018) that gross inequality of wealth produces ill-health and social instability for all eventually, but it is the poorest who are suffering disproportionately at the hands of Covid-19. Thomas Piketty (2014) in his encyclopaedic 'Capitalism in the 21st Century' argues for taxation on an international scale. I sometimes feel that the rich liars who sold Brexit to the British people are motivated by fear of the EU at last beginning to close in on their tax havens.

We have tried austerity and harsh welfare reforms in the UK. It has been a disaster just as your Yanis Varoufakis said it would be. We know that societies moving rapidly in this direction are not happy places – the world has Trump, the British have Brexit, Boris Johnson and Dominic Cummings, and Europe has Hungary, Poland, Austria and now Italy. Who knows what Brazil will add to the cocktail. More walls, nationalism, xenophobia and racism.

But Varoufakis is also an optimist. He says "I have a very deep respect in the capacity of human minds to work things out for themselves – so long as they do not have to live in terror." Sounds to me like a pretty good justification for democratic education.

If governments can find a minimum of rationality, which I am pleased to see growing in the English opposition Labour Party now led by Keir Starmer, they will turn to Universal Basic Income (UBI) (Standing, 2017) to achieve some kind of social stability as paid employment declines. All around the world there are a growing number of pilot schemes for UBI, some supported by wealthy silicon-valley entrepreneurs such as Sam Altman of Combinator. These show that wealth, if regarded as a kind of commons that has been created by past generations rather than by hedge funds, can be shared as a basic income for all. When this happens, there is a widespread feeling of equity, social justice and well-being, a reduction in economic insecurity, and a growth in social, political and economic entrepreneurial activism. All aspects of a good society.

After all it is well known that much of the wealth of the super-rich has actually come from publicly funded research. It is only right that some of it should be shared unconditionally to provide basic income for all humanity as a human right. This could at last set people free with the time to pursue activities of their own choice. Unemployment from paid labour would no longer be a self-diminishing curse but an opportunity – to start a society, to become active in a political group, or to play music or paint pictures – as one of my own sons has done. After years of struggle his paintings are now selling and he is paying a significant amount of tax. Something the mega-rich need to be prepared to do!

But – for Universal Basic Income to work people will have to be able to take responsibility for their own lives and be able to create their own identity and meaning. They will have to stop relying on employers and paid employment to define their identity. Secure paid labour that will last unchanged for many years already no longer exists for the majority of people.

People will have to be able to redefine work as what they want to do with their lives. To do what they are good at. To create community with others who also know how to manage their own time. People who can reflect and participate as active citizens in democracies, both local direct democracies, and regional or national indirect or representative democracies. All with a deep understanding of human rights and respect for diversity.

These democracies will be under threat from demagogues like Trump and Putin. They will have easy answers as to who is to blame for the uncertainties that surround us – the Roma, the Jews, the immigrants, the homeless, the disabled etc. etc. To resist their nostrums and snake-oil we will need a young generation deeply grounded and experienced in respect for democracy and human rights.

Well – I ask you – what kind of schools already exist that know how to nurture such young people, to provide the soil for such people to grow? What kind of schools are going to be needed for all young people if the planet is to have a future?

Exactly!! The bi-pillared democratic schools! Schools where young people are learning to construct their own identities, where they can make time their own to discover and deepen their interests and celebrate their creativity and curiosity while developing competences that are meaningful to them – who do not rely on others to instruct them and tell them what to do and when to do it. This is for sure where the 1-2% needed to create and develop the technology of the Fourth Industrial Revolution will be found. And if they have been to democratic schools they will hopefully have the necessary ethical values to recognise and support the rights of all to a fully realised life.

And what about the other 98%? For them, or 'us' should I say, it will be even more important that they have learned to collaborate in democratic rights respecting schools where they can develop the will, understanding and determination to ensure that this new wave of technology benefits and liberates humanity and does not destroy us all; to ensure that it is subject to the democratic control of people who have the time and the capacity to think for themselves.

If we don't change our schools there is a real danger of insurrection as millions find themselves ill-equipped to deal with the new uncertainties despite the best efforts of those advocating a gift economy, or a sharing economy, or a circular economy – all of which I approve. Here are some dystopian thoughts. In the US there are some 3.5 million truck drivers. They are a well-paid working-class elite most of whom own guns and support Trump. Over the next 5-10 years much of their work will disappear as trucks become automated self-driving vehicles. Who will Trump and his ilk tell them to blame?

This will happen in many occupations. Already computers make more accurate diagnoses than most medical doctors because they can review so many case histories so quickly. When secure crypto-currencies replace banking where will the millions of bank clerks go – and where will the Uber drivers go when taxis are driverless, and the Deliveroo riders when drones deliver our pizzas. If we are not careful, we will fall victim to what Darrell West calls 'Trumpism on steroids.'

It seems to me that as a progressive democratic-schools movement we can either retreat into the woods with our small happy schools and hope that the 'real world' will forget about us and go away. We can take up 'folk politics' leaving the woods from time to time to occupy Times Square until we get bored and go home having changed nothing. We can become 'survivalists' without guns.

Or we can say welcome to a world where much meaningless paid labour will end and become much more willing to engage with the public and the public school systems, the media, mainstream politicians and policy makers to explain to them what kind of social policies, such as universal basic income, will be required for a sustainable democratic world to emerge and survive. And surely it is our special task to be willing to explain what kind of schools will be required for all our children to be able to thrive in that world. We need to stop being so shy about the fact THAT THESE SCHOOLS ALREADY EXIST!

The neo-liberals planned their successful bid for world hegemony for their ideas very carefully. It was no accident that they overwhelmed Keynesianism in a decade. I think we need to do the same – to make the same effort – building on the proven success of our small-scale democratic school models, we need to make the case for the democratisation of our public/state school systems. We need to imagine short, medium, and long-term goals as the neo-liberals did. We need to ask 'what would a national democratic school system look like?'

Perhaps the biggest lesson that I have learned, is the importance of not being alone. I think our potential power is something like the mathematical square of the size of our group of like minds. As the song says 'one is one and all alone and ever more shall be so' whereas two have the strength of four, three as nine, etc etc. Find some friends. Choose them carefully – then study the behaviour of the fox!! There is always something that can be done. Teachers in the Ukraine, unlike teachers in my country, have a government with a policy framework that wants you to be innovative, to create a new and better way.

We must resist the dystopian Orwellian future that the Belorussian writer Evgeny Morozov describes as 'digital feudalism.' In this version of the future elites will be able to use artificial intelligence to extend and maintain their wealth and position. In alliance with authoritarian states and with the right algorithms, they will keep tighter and tighter control over the innermost thoughts and behaviours of the rest of us. A fear of the ideas of Xi Jin Ping is driving the young people onto the streets of Hong Kong right now. You could almost see our current authoritarian school systems as perfect preparation for this future.

We have an opportunity to align ourselves with the Council of Europe's 'Democratic Schools for All' project – which EUDEC (European Democratic

Education Community) has begun to do. One of Germany's democratic schools (Netzwerk Schule, Berlin) has attended an Oslo conference with progressive state schools from around Europe. EUDEC has a real role to play in this challenge to communicate. It has been exciting and encouraging that EUDEC was invited to join the advisory board of a major academic project involving 15 universities and 15 NGOs led by the University of the Basque Country. It is the 'To Share' project which would involve collating and reviewing projects from around Europe which are already beginning to address the challenges of the Fourth Industrial Revolution. It would then recommend policies by which democratic politics could get some control over the technology involved.

EUDEC was identified by the 'To Share' coordinators as an organisation with something unique to say. Sadly, the EU did not fund the project this year, but there will be another application next year and hopefully EUDEC will maintain its commitment to the idea.

I believe that another way is possible. If we succeed, we can make creative use of the immense increases in productivity and free time offered by the Fourth Industrial Revolution. We can adopt the ideas of the circular and sharing economies to create more equitable, humanly fulfilling, and environmentally sustainable societies that are grounded in democracy and human rights. We can use the productivity of artificial intelligence rather than be used by it. We can delay technological singularity for ever. We can focus on things like empathy and compassion which it cannot emulate. Democratic education can and will help us to achieve this – I think we really have no choice – I have to be an optimist despite my age – I have seven grandchildren! We need not just the new Ukrainian School but the new European School and the new International school. A new kind of school for planet Earth. Nothing is more important.

So, others are beginning to recognise the importance of our existence and our message. Let's amplify our voices to ensure that we communicate more effectively. In this 'age of disruption' let's think hard about how we can 'disrupt' our national school systems. Most of them desperately need it!

Thanks for a wonderful conference!

Derry Hannam. 2018/2019

NOTES

(1) Secondary modern schools were one part of the tri-partite selective school system that developed in England following the 1944 English Education Act. The 'top' 10-30% of eleven year-olds were selected in the 11+ test for grammar school academic pre-university education. The percentage of places varied widely from locality to locality. A further 20% were supposed to be selected for technical school education but in most parts of the country these schools were never built. The remainder were selected for secondary modern schools where the education would be in inferior buildings and of a 'practical' nature. The intelligence tests used in the 11+ are almost completely discredited as both invalid and unreliable yet they are still in use in a few parts of the country.

(2) OFSTED – The Office for Standards In Education. The current school inspection system for England

(3) Prep or preparatory schools. These are expensive private often residential schools in England to which wealthy families (7%) send their younger children up to the age of 13 prior to attendance at public (expensive, elite, private) schools.

(4) Sixth Forms are to be found mainly in public, grammar and comprehensive schools for students aged 16-18 who have completed the 16+ GCSE examinations and are working towards A level 18+ pre-university examinations. Secondary Modern schools often do not have Sixth Forms as students commonly leave school at 16. The school of 1H/2H did have a Sixth Form however.

(5) Prefects are older students almost always appointed by the head teacher to assist the teachers in disciplining the rest of the students. They are most commonly to be found in public schools and grammar or comprehensive schools trying to imitate public schools.

(6) The cane was an implement for the infliction of corporal punishment on the hand or the buttocks. Widely used in English secondary schools until banned by law in 1987. The author was caned four times at his grammar school – on no occasion had he committed the alleged offence!

(7) O levels refers to the 'Ordinary Level' of the GCSE subject examinations usually taken at the age of 16 year

BIBLIOGRAPHY

Acemoglu, D., Robinson, J.A., and Verdier, T. (2012) Can't We All Be More Like Scandinavians. Asymmetric Growth and Institutions in an Interdependent World (NBER Working Paper No. 18441). Cambridge, Mass.: National Bureau of Economic Research (NBER).

Babkin, B.P. (1949) Pavlov, A Biography. Chicago: University of Chicago Press.

Baginsky, M. and Hannam, D.H. (1999) School Councils, The Views of Students and Teachers. London: NSPCC.

Boaler, J. (1997) Experiencing School Mathematics: Teaching Styles, Sex, and Setting. Buckingham: Open University Press.

Boaler, J. (2013) Ability and Mathematics: the Mindset Revolution that is Reshaping Education. Forum Vol. 55, Number 1.

Boeke, K. (1945) Sociocracy: Democracy as it Might Be. Online at worldteacher.faithweb.com/sociocracy.com.htm.

Bregman, R. (2020) Humankind. A Hopeful History. London: Bloomsbury.

Bruner, J.S. (1960) The Process of Education. Boston: Harvard University Press.

Bruner, J.S. (1966) Towards a Theory of Instruction. Boston: Harvard University Press.

Butterworth, J. (1932) Clubland. London: The Epworth Press.

Cadwell, L. (1997) Bringing Reggio Emilia Home. An Innovative Approach to Early Childhood Education. New York: Teachers College Press.

Carnie, F (2018) Rebuilding Our Schools from the Bottom Up. London: Routledge.

Clay, D., Gold, J., and Hannam, D.H. (2001) Secondary School Councils Toolkit. Students and Teachers Working Together. London: School Councils UK.

Council of Europe (1950) European Convention on Human Rights

(ECHR). Strasbourg: Council of Europe Publishing.

Council of Europe (2003) COMPASS. A Manual on Human Rights Education with Young People. Strasbourg: Council of Europe Publishing.

Crick, B et.al. (1998) Education for Citizenship and the Teaching of Democracy in Schools. London: Quality and Curriculum Authority (QCA).

Cunningham, I., et.al. (2000) Report of an Inquiry into Summerhill School. Brighton: Centre For Self-Managed Learning.

Curry, W.B. (1934) The School. London: John Lane.

Davies, L., and Yamashita, H. (2007) School Councils. School Improvement. Birmingham: Centre for International Education and Research (CIER) – The University of Birmingham.

Economist Intelligence Unit (2020) Staff of 2030: Future Ready Teaching. London: The Economist.

Fielding, M. (2011) Student Voice and the Possibility of Radical Democratic Education: Re-narrating Forgotten Histories. Developing Alternative Futures. In G. Czerniawski and W. Kidd (Eds.), The Student Voice Handbook. Bingley: Emerald Group.

Fielding, M. and Bragg, S. (2003) Students as Researchers: Making a Difference. London: Pearson Publishing.

Freire, P. (1970) Pedagogy of the Opressed. New York: Continuum.

Gilligan, C (1982) In a Different Voice. Psychological Theory and Women's Development. Cambridge, Mass.: Harvard University Press.

Golding, W. (1954). Lord of the Flies. London: Faber and Faber.

Gray, P. (2013) Free to Learn. Why Unleashing the Instinct to Play will make Our Children Happier, More Self-Reliant, and Better Students for Life. New York: Basic Books.

Greenberg, D., et.al. (1992) The Sudbury Valley School Experience. Framingham: The Sudbury Valley School Press.

Habermas, J (1962, tr. English 1989) The Structural Transformation of the Public Sphere. Berlin: Luchterhand.

Hallgarten, J., Breslin, T., and Hannam D.H. (2004) I Was A Teenage Governo: Project Report Phase 1. London: IPPR.

Hannam, D.H. (1999) Biodiversity or Monoculture. The need for

Alternatives and Diversity in the School System. Keynote speech at the International Democratic Education Conference (IDEC) held at Summerhill School, 23rd-26th July, 1999.

Hannam, D.H. (2001) A Pilot Study to Evaluate the Impact of the Student Participation Aspects of Citizenship Order on Standards of Education in Secondary Schools. London: CSV.

Hannam, D.H. (2005) I Was A Teenage Governor: Project Report Phase 2. London:Citizenship Foundation.

Hannam, D.H. (2011) A Review of Recent Research into Children's Rights Based Education in State Schools in Hampshire, England. Leipzig, Germany: EUDEC.

Hannam, P. and Echevarria, E. (2009) Philosophy With Teenagers: Nurturing a Moral Imagination for the Twenty-First Century. London: Continuum.

Holzman, l. and Newman, F. (1993) Lev Vygotsky Revolutionary Scientist. London: Routledge.

Hopkin, J.L., Lapuente, V., and Moller, L. (2014) Lower Levels Of Inequality Are Linked With Greater Innovation in Economics (blog entry). London: London School of Economics. (http://bit.ly/1jPOV6A).

Kohlberg, L. and Higgins, A. (1987) School Democracy and Social Interaction. In Kirtine, W.M. and Gewirtz, J.L., (eds.) Moral Development Through Social Interaction. New York: Wiley.

Kohn, A. (1999) The Schools Our Children Deserve. Boston: Houghton Mifflin.

Kohn, A. (2013) In conversation with the author at AERO conference, Long Island University, New York, May 13-19, 2013.

Lane, H. (1928) Talks to Parents and Teachers. London: Allen and Unwin.

Lipman (2003) Thinking in Education. Cambridge: Cambridge University Press.

Maslow, A. (1954) Motivation and Personality. New York: Harper.

Meadows, D.H. (1972) Limits to Growth. New York: Universe Books.

Mercogliano, C. (1998) Making It Up As We Go Along; The Story of the Albany Free School. Portsmouth (NH): Heinemann.

Mosley, J. and Murray, P. (1996) Quality Circle Time in the Primary

Classroom. London: David Fulton Publishers.

OECD (2009) Programme for International Student Assessment (PISA). Paris: OECD.

Office for Standards in Education (Osted). (2003) The Education of Six Year Olds in England, Denmark and Finland. London: Ofsted.

Pekkarrinen, T., Uusitolo, R., Pekkala, S. (2006) Education Policy and Intergenerational Income Mobility; Evidence from the Finnish Comprehensive School Reform. Discussion Paper 2204. Bonn: IZA (Institute for the Study of Labour).

Piketty, T. (2014) Capital In the Twenty-First Century. Cambridge, Mass.: Belknap-Harvard University Press

Popper, K. (1945) The Open Society and its Enemies. London: Routledge.

Poster, C. (1982) Community Education. Its Development and Management. New York: Barnes and Noble.

Potter, J. (2002) Active Citizenship In Schools. London: Kogan Page.

QCA – Qualifications and Curriculum Agency (2000) National Curriculum Citizenship at Key Stages 3 and 4. Initial Guidance for Schools. London: Qualifications and Curriculum Agency.

Rawson, W. (1956) The Werkplaats Adventure. London: Vincent Stuart.

Ree, H. (1971) Educator Extraordinary: The Life and Achievements of Henry Morris. London: Longman.

Rudduck, J. and McIntyre, D. (2007) Improving Learning through Consulting Pupils. London: Routledge.

Russell, B. (1926) On Education. London: Allen and Unwin.

Russell, B (1946) History of Western Philosophy. London: Allen and Unwin.

Sahlberg, P. (2013) Finnish Lessons 2.0. What can the World learn from educational change in Finland. New York: Teacher's College Press.

Semler, R. (1988) Maverick. New York: Warner Books.

Semler, R. (2003) The Seven Day Weekend. London: Random House.

Sharp, J. (1973) Open School. London: J.M. Dent and sons.

Shor, I. (1996) When Students Have Power. Negotiating Authority in a

Critical Pedagogy. Chicago: University of Chicago Press.

Simpson, J.H. (1954) Schoolmaster's Harvest. London: Faber and Faber.

Skinner, B.F. (1968) The Technology of Teaching. New York: Appleton.

Srnicek, N., and Williams, A. (2015) Inventing the Future. London: Verso.

Standing, G. (2017) Basic Income: And How We Can Make It Happen. London: Pelican Books.

Suffolk County Council (1999) A Report on Summerhill School. Ipswich: Suffolk County Council Social Services Department.

Torney-Purta, J. (1999 and 2001) Citizenship and Education in Twenty-Eight Countries: Civic Knowledge and Engagement at Age Fourteen. Amsterdam: IEA (International Association for the Evaluation of Educational Achievement).

United Nations (1948) Universal Declaration of Human Rights. New York: United Nations.

United Nations (1989) Convention on the Rights of the Child. New York: United Nations.

Watts, J (1977) The Countesthorpe Experience. London: Allen and Unwin.

Wilkinson, R., and Pickett, K. (2010) The Spirit Level. Why Equality is Better for Everyone. London: Penguin Books.

Wilkinson, R., and Pickett, K. (2018) The Inner Level. How More Equal Societies Reduce Stress, Restore Sanity and improve Everyone's Well-being. London: Penguin Random House.

Wills, W.D. (1964) Homer Lane, A Biography. London: Allen and Unwin.

Winnicott, D.W. (1971) Playing and Reality. London: Tavistock Publications.

Winnicott, D.W. (1973) The Child, the Family, and the Outside World. Reading, Mass.: De Capo Press.

Wojcicki, E. (2019) How to Raise Successful People. London: Hutchinson.

***

FHREE

FULL HUMAN RIGHTS-EXPERIENCE EDUCATION

Printed in Great Britain
by Amazon